Richard Peace is a professional freelance writer and photographer. Born in 1966, he was educated at Queen Elizabeth Grammar School, Wakefield and Magdalen College, Oxford, obtaining a degree in Modern History before qualifying as a solicitor. His passion for writing combined with his great enthusiasm for places, people and travel have led to the publication of his six previous books. He is also a regular contributor to numerous magazines.

He currently lives in Wakefield, West Yorkshire, and when not working he is often found travelling abroad, researching and writing. His hobbies include book collecting and languages.

Following page
The Pigeon Tower, Lever Park (see no 37)

Lancashire Curiosities

Richard Peace

THE DOVECOTE PRESS

First published in 1997 by The Dovecote Press Ltd
Stanbridge, Wimborne, Dorset BH21 4JD

ISBN 1 874336 42 3

© Richard Peace 1997

Typeset by The Typesetting Bureau, Wimborne, Dorset
Printed and bound in Great Britain by
Baskerville Press Ltd, Salisbury, Wiltshire

1   3   5   7   9   8   6   4   2

Contents

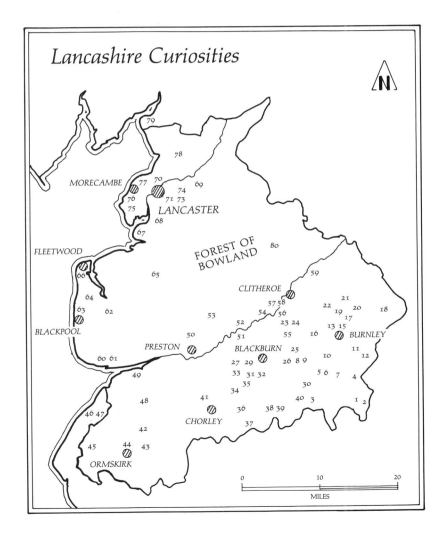

Introduction

Do you want to know more about the enigmatic traces the past has left on modern-day Lancashire? Have you ever wondered about strange-looking buildings or monuments? Such curiosities often prompt people to ask 'what is that?' or 'why is it there?'. This book is an attempt to provide answers, and all the 'curiosities' I have included either have some distinguishing feature or an unusual tale attached to them.

Lancashire's geography and history are, of course, reflected in the curiosities themselves. Occasionally the modern county boundary is crossed into areas that have traditionally considered themselves Lancastrian. From the hill country of Burnley and Blackburn, an industrial heartland, to the largely agricultural Fylde plain and quintessentially English seaside resorts reminders of bygone days exist. Some may be nationally famous, such as Blackpool Tower, whilst others are virtually unknown and hard to find, such as the 'Wet Tower' near Ramsbottom. Some can be driven right up to in a car, whilst a handful lie on lonely moors and need time, preparation and a stout pair of walking boots. Most are easily accessible, but any potential restrictions such as opening hours or admission charges are mentioned. Curiosities in churches are best visited on a Sunday as many are locked mid-week. Full details are given to enable the curiosity-seeker to find his or her chosen curiosity, always with reference to the appropriate Landranger 1:50,000 map.

Many of the curiosities are, at the time of writing, in excellent condition and some are still lived in or used. Although many are listed buildings, such protection is no guarantee of immortality. Nature or mindless vandalism may be just as much a threat as thoughtless development, as is obvious from the state of some of the curiosities. If this guide encourages an interest in such sites less careful owners will hopefully come to realise that they are guardians of the county's heritage, which if it disappears will be lost both to us and to future generations forever.

Acknowledgements

This book could not have been completed without a great deal of help from many people. David Burnett at the Dovecote Press was enthusiastic about the project from start to finish and various individuals from numerous organisations clearly shared my own interest in the unusual architecture and hidden corners of their county, often far beyond the call of duty.

A special debt is owed to Spectrum Colour Library, for the photograph of Blackpool Tower, and John Champness, Lancashire County Council Conservation Officer for providing illustrations of India Mill, Ormskirk Water Tower and Arnside Tower.

I am grateful to the following: The staff of the local studies libraries in Rawtenstall, Lancaster, Darwen, Ormskirk, Blackburn, Ramsbottom and Southport; John Champness, County Conservation Officer; Maggy Simms, Blackburn Museum and Art Galleries; Judith Douglas, Blackburn Borough Council; Mick Onley, Rossendale Borough Council; Tania Hyndell, Hyndburn Borough Council; Reverend D. H. Hughes, St. Bartholomew's Church, Whitworth; John Spencer, Herbal Health, Rawtenstall; those providing information at Burnley Borough Council, Towneley Hall Art Gallery and Museums; Arthur Giddins, Bacup Natural History Museum. Brotherly support in the form of Robert's proof-reading and David's assistance with photo development was also a huge help.

1. Gargoyles with Character

Position: Whitworth, north of Rochdale
O.S.Map: Landranger, Manchester, Sheet 109
Map Ref: 887 176
Access: Pass through Whitworth on the A671. Look for the Dog and
Partridge pub and go up Church Street keeping left up Taylor Street.
Split off left into Whitworth Square (parking possible).

St. Bartholomew's Church at Whitworth has some highly individual
gargoyles. Most noticeable is the profusion of carvings on the tower; in
particular look out for the highly expressive howling dog. Others are
more specific, especially the group found on the end wall away from
the tower. Easily identified is the figure bearing a child in his arms. This
is said to be 'Owd Barnes', who supposedly went every day to the
church during its construction to monitor its progress (another theory
is that he was actually a stone mason who worked there). He was
known for his unusual looks and unconventional dress sense, sometimes turning up wearing a clog on one foot and a shoe on the other.
Other gargoyles mentioned in the records are likenesses of the original
vicar and his son and Mr. Edmund Lord, a singer at the Whitworth Chapel for 70 years, although these examples are harder to
identify with certainty. A more biblical theme is reflected in the
carved emblems on the east side of the tower which all relate to the
Crucifixion. Over the west door look out for the highly unusual
carving of a dragon and a woman holding a spear. This is perhaps a
reference to events described in Genesis.

The church was finished in 1850 at a cost of £4,500, a sum that
impoverished its principal benefactor, the Rev. Isaac Gaitskell. It owes
its anomalous proportions to a fire in 1984. As much of the old church
as possible was salvaged and incorporated into a new plan. Many of
the gargoyles were moved from the sides to the end in the rebuilding
process.

Places of Interest in the Neighbourhood
  2. Doctors Galore
  4. An Aladdin's Cave
 76. A Grave Concern

The carving of 'Owd Barnes', Whitworth.

2. Doctors Galore

Position: Whitworth, just north of Rochdale
O.S.Map: Landranger, Manchester, Sheet 109
Map Ref: 886 176
Access: Whitworth Square. For directions to the square see entry 1.

Whitworth Square was once the centre of a bizarre medical practice based round James Taylor, who opened his practice in 1764. 26 members of the Taylor family went on to practice medicine in the town, the last of them dying in 1876.

It was not just the size of the medical family that attracted attention but its excruciating-sounding 'cures'. Some of the patients who came for treatment (the better-off staying at what is now the Red Lion pub) never left alive! One of the Taylors' remedies was *keen*, a caustic ointment said to 'cure' cancers and growths. The Taylors' behaviour was often less than conventional; the Bishop of Durham was abandoned during treatment when a sick horse took priority, although this becomes less surprising when we learn the doctor in question originally trained as a vet! The graveyard on the hillside contains a monolith in memory of the Taylor family.

Places of Interest in the Neighbourhood
  1. Gargoyles with Character
  4. An Aladdin's Cave
76. A Grave Concern

The Taylor family memorial, Whitworth.

3. The Wet Tower

Position: Stubbins near Ramsbottom
O.S.Map: Landranger, Manchester, Sheet 109
Map Ref: 788 184
Access: Head north on the A676 through Stubbins. Go left (dead end) just before the rail bridge and up Stubbins Street then right at a T-junction by terraced houses. Bear to the right of Stubbins Fold (car access ends). Follow the track until you reach the tower.

The Wet Tower's intriguing name hints at its former purpose. Stubbins Vale Mill is now largely demolished, but in its heyday it produced a variety of textiles for the printing industry such as filter fabrics, printing blankets and felts used in the production of hand-made paper. Many of them went to the Wet Tower in the final stages of production. The fabrics were laid out on the field or stretched on tenter frames then, whilst still wet, they were hung from the top storey. Finally the building was sealed and the textiles fumigated with sulphur candles.

Places of Interest in the Neighbourhood
30. A Penny a Pot
38. Defensive Tower or Industrialist's Fancy?
39. Legacies of the Steam Age
40. Two Lonely Monuments

The Wet Tower, near Ramsbottom.

4.   An Aladdin's Cave

Position: Bacup
O.S.Map: Landranger, Blackburn and Burnley, Sheet 103. Town
centre map useful.
Map Ref: 868 233
Access: On Yorkshire Street in Bacup town centre, just off the A681.

The story of this eclectic collection of objects is almost as interesting
as the collection itself. In the latter half of the 19th century a small
group of locals with an interest in the natural history of the locality
responded in competitive style to the fact that nearby Haslingden had
its own museum.

Today the Bacup Natural History Society is still going strong and
boasts a lecture theatre, library, study and museum which together
house thousands of objects, photographs, books and newspapers as a
testament to a past age. The society expanded from its natural history base to include many other areas of interest; the museum now
houses Victoriana and bygones of all types as well as collections of
stuffed animals, birds' eggs, fossils, industrial archaeology, mining and
quarrying artefacts along with military relics and much more besides,
all built up from the collecting enthusiasm of members or donations.
The premises are opened during society meetings on Thursdays, 7-9.30
p.m.

Places of Interest in the Neighbourhood
1. Gargoyles with Character
2. Doctors Galore
7. The Slipper King

5. Britain's Last Temperance Bar

Position: Rawtenstall
O.S.Map: Landranger, Blackburn and Burnley, Sheet 103. Town centre map also useful.
Map Ref: 814 228
Access: Rawtenstall Town Centre, Bank St.

'Herbal Health' may, at a cursory glance, appear to be just another health food shop, but in reality it is the last remaining temperance bar in Britain. An original marble and mahogany counter stands in the corner, topped by a large copper water heater. Exotic brews such as Black Beer and Raisin, Vitalo Tonic, Blood Tonic and Sarsaparilla and Liquorice, made to late 19th century recipes, can be bought by the pint or the glass. They are still concocted on the premises and stored in beautiful earthenware casks behind the counter. On surrounding shelves you will also come across old glass jars full of such exotic herbs and spices as skull cap, red sage and wormwood.

The temperance bar, Rawtenstall.

The bar is a reminder of an age when such institutions, designed to 'save' Lancashire workers from the 'demon booze', were a common feature of the industrial landscape. The origin of the recipes can be dated back at least to the father of Malachi Fitzpatrick, an Irish immigrant, who founded a chain of temperance bars in the Lancashire mill towns of the 1890's and discovered a ready market on the back of the teetotal movement. One wonders what the original customers would make of today's goings on there; prior to use as a temperance bar it was, ironically, a pub called the 'One Too Many'!

Places of Interest in the Neighbourhood
  4. An Aladdin's Cave
  6. A Cottage with a Purpose
  7. The Slipper King
 30. A Penny a Pot

The 'Weavers' Cottage', Rawtenstall.

6. A Cottage with a Purpose

Position: Rawtenstall town centre
O.S.Map: Landranger, Blackburn and Burnley, Sheet 103
Map Ref: 814 227
Access: Opposite the cricket ground on the Bacup road, just outside the town centre. Contact (01706) 229828 / 229937 for opening details.

This rare 'weavers' cottage' represents a time in the 18th century when textile production was in a state of transformation between cottage and factory industry.

The most notable feature of the exterior is the amazing number of close set, mullioned windows on the second and third storeys. Here the maximum light was required by the spinners who gathered together to take advantage of the dry, airy atmosphere. Despite working in a group they still retained their skilled and independent status; they had not yet become mere machine minders. Raw material was supplied using the restored 'taking in' door on the top storey.

The cottage was erected around 1780 for cloth weaving and is seen today more or less as it would have been when used to manufacture baize by Richard Ashworth. It was saved from demolition by Rawtenstall Civic Society who now open it on weekend afternoons, Easter to September. Inside are a spinning wheel, handloom, Victorian kitchen and cloggers shop.

Places of Interest in the Neighbourhood
4. An Aladdin's Cave
5. Britain's Last Temperance Bar
7. The Slipper King
30. A Penny a Pot

7. The Slipper King

Position: Waterfoot near Rawtenstall
O.S.Map: Landranger, Blackburn and Burnley, Sheet 103
Map Ref: 835 219
Access: The Footwear Museum is at Gaghills Mill, on the B6238, just
north of Waterfoot, between Rawtenstall and Bacup. Open 10 a.m.-
5.30 p.m. Monday-Friday, 9.30 a.m.-3.30 p.m. Saturdays.

This quaint, little footwear museum houses such exotica as slippers
decorated with ibis feathers or rabbit fur and shoes designed for
Buckingham Palace servants. The collection is in the old boardroom of
H.W.Trickett, slipper manufacturers, and is alongside a shoe mill
shop.

The unusual collection is much more than a trip through the history
of shoe style and manufacture as it reflects the overbearing influence of
one man on the huge shoe industry that sprung up around the Irwell
Valley in the nineteenth and twentieth centuries. H.W.Trickett began
manufacturing slippers aged twenty six in 1883. By the time of his
death in 1913 his factory employed 1,200 people and annually turned
out two-and-a-half million pairs of footwear. Its owner was known the
world over as the 'Slipper King', and his workers' gratitude is still
commemorated by the memorial clock above the arcade that fronts the
Rawtenstall-Bacup road.

Today the footwear company owning the mill employs around 1,350
people and produces 5 million pairs of footwear a year.

Places of Interest in the Neighbourhood
4. An Aladdin's Cave
5. Britain's Last Temperance Bar
6. A Cottage with a Purpose

8. Pals to the End

Position: Accrington
O.S.Map: Landranger, Blackburn and Burnley, Sheet 103 and town centre map
Map Ref: 759 286 and various sites near the town centre
Access: The town centre has plenty of car parking and a central train station.

Whilst many towns tuck their war memorial away in a quiet corner it seems difficult to avoid the ghosts of the First World War wherever one turns in Accrington. Shortly after the 1914 war began Lord Kitchener formed 'pals' units, or men formed into companies based on the district they came from. It was thought local bonds would give them greater cohesion and fighting spirit.

Initially the Accrington Pals trained at various locations around town and were a familiar sight. It was, however, events in France that gave many of the places in Accrington associated with the Pals such tragic poignancy. On July 1st 1916, 100,000 British troops advanced along a fifteen mile front at the start of the Battle of the Somme. It took the Pals only twenty minutes to sustain 235 dead and 350 injured out of a total of 700.

Numerous places in the town have some link with the Pals. The Pals Memorial Chapel at St. John the Evangelist Church (on Addison Street off Burnley Road) is open 9.00 a.m. - 5.00 p.m. daily, whilst the regiment's colours, awarded to them in February 1919, are in St. James Church between Willow and Cannon Street near the town centre. In the coppice at the top of Avenue Parade there is still evidence of the trenches dug by the Pals during training. Other buildings also retain associations. Ellison's Tenement was used for marching practice whilst the former tram shed (now Hyndburn Transport Bus Depot) was used in wet weather. When the Pals left Accrington in 1915, 16,000 people lined the streets to watch them march off to war.

A useful leaflet on the Accrington Pals Trail is available from the Information Centre in the Town Hall.

Places of Interest in the Neighbourhood
9. A Musical Enigma
25. A Fêted Son
26. 'Fairy Caves' of Early Industry

9. A Musical Enigma

Position: Accrington town centre
O.S.Map: Landranger, Blackburn and Burnley, Sheet 103
Map Ref: 759 284
Access: The tomb of Adam Westwell is near the St. James Street entrance to St. James churchyard near Accrington town centre.

The carved object that stands on the tomb of Adam Westwell has aroused more controversy than the tomb's occupant. It is an unusual and little known musical instrument, an ophicleide (spelt wrongly on the tomb). According to those who knew him, Adam Westwell was the finest ophicleide player in Lancashire and played with the Accrington Old Band. Indeed, the band thought sufficiently of him to have the carving erected in his honour.

The ophicleide (an early form of tuba) was heavy and cumbersome and needed an immense amount of 'puff' to produce a note. Adam Westwell's own fate was rather more tragic. After touring with Wombwell's Wild Beast Show, he returned home in 1859. An acquaintance of Westwell is recorded as saying that he was, at this time, 'a complete wreck, both in mind and in body' and that he had come home to die. Whilst in this deranged state he tried to participate in the organisation of the opening ceremony of a civic building, blowing out only 'dismal notes' and he died shortly afterwards.

Places of Interest in the Neighbourhood
 8. Pals to the End
25. A Fêted Son
26. 'Fairy Caves' of Early Industry

The monument to Adam Westwell, Accrington.

10. An Open-Air Baptistery

Position: Near Clowbridge Reservoir, between Burnley and
Rawtenstall
O.S.Map: Landranger, Blackburn and Burnley, Sheet 103
Map Ref: 828 277
Access: From Clowbridge Reservoir Car Park follow the waymarked
Gambleside Trail south of the reservoir. The open-air baptistery is
about half a mile along the trail.

Gambleside was once a thriving hamlet, high on the moorland of the
Forest of Rossendale. Although most of the former buildings decayed
or were demolished sometime after the building of a reservoir in 1866,
a rare open-air baptistery remains.

Gambleside was strategically placed on a packhorse route used for
carrying wool and, from the 16th century on, coal. By the mid-
nineteenth century coal was being produced from two main shafts and
the hamlet consisted of a farmhouse, the Mansion House, a cottage, a
barn and a Baptist Chapel. The open-air baptistery was connected to
the chapel and is now one of the few remnants of this remote community. It resembles a small stone-lined swimming pool, and has a
small set of steps for descending into the water. It was extended to
almost twice its original size in order to double up as a water supply for
the steam engine which extracted water from one of the mining shafts,
and was recently restored by North West Water.

The Baptists (originally Anabaptists) were distinguished from other
Protestant sects by their emphasis on baptism. They believed baptism
should be administered only to believers, infant baptism alone being
insufficient, and that full immersion was necessary; not an enticing
prospect on these windy heights, even in summer!

Places of Interest in the Neighbourhood
5. Britain's Last Temperance Bar
6. A Cottage with a Purpose
13. Steam Power
14. A Catholic Retreat
15. The Canal Town

11. Literary Corners

Position: Hurstwood hamlet near Burnley
O.S.Map: Landranger, Blackburn and Burnley, Sheet 103
Map Ref: 882 314
Access: To the east of Burnley, Hurstwood hamlet lies off the
Mereclough-Worsthorne road.

Spenser's cottage lies in an almost idyllic setting opposite the
Elizabethan Hurstwood Hall in a hamlet surrounding the River Brun.
It was the home of the Spenser family, until they moved to London.
The famous Elizabethan poet, Edmund, retired here in 1576 and it
allegedly gave him the inspiration to write *The Faerie Queen*. More
certainly it inspired a poem in honour of his Rosalind, possibly Rose
Dinely of Clitheroe. Beyond Spenser's cottage is Tattersall's Tenement, site of Richard Tattersall's first horse sale. He went on to
establish the world famous stables.

Equally inspiring is Lindeth Tower at Silverdale (map ref: 461 742)
where the Victorian novelist Mrs. Gaskell spent many hours. Mrs.
Gaskell's 'discovery' of the Silverdale coastal area in the 1850s led to a

Lindeth Tower, Silverdale.

great surge in its popularity, not surprising given the area's unique combination of limestone knolls, expansive views across Morecambe Bay, salt flats and drystone walls. It stands several stories high. Like Spenser's cottage it is in private ownership but is easily visible from the road.

Less well known is the Lancastrian dialect writer, Edwin Waugh, who is commemorated on the lonely Scout Moor by a bronze figurehead above a spring (map ref: 829 199 sheet 109). Known as 'The Burns of Lancashire', he was born at Rochdale in 1817 and died at New Brighton in 1890. He often stayed at nearby Fo Edge Farm and it is thought he mused over his ideas by this spring. His works include 'Come Home to thi Childer an' Me', extolling the virtues of domestic life, and 'I've Worn My Bits o' Shoon Away' on the attractions of the east Lancashire moorland. He also produced a standard simpler form of Lancashire dialect, many of whose words and phrases are still in use. He was also a successful writer of poetry and travel books in standard English.

Places of Interest in the Neighbourhood
12. A Lost Industry
13. Steam Power
14. A Catholic Retreat
15. The Canal Town

Old lime workings, Shedden Clough.

12. A Lost Industry

Position: Shedden Clough near Burnley
O.S.Map: Landranger, Blackburn and Burnley, Sheet 103
Map Ref: 895 295
Access: Head east out of Burnley and on to the Long Causeway, the
minor road north of the A646 in the Calder Valley. About 7 kilometres
from Burnley town centre there is an isolated car park next to Shedden
Hushings, next to the wind generators.

Before the large-scale production and transport of lime for building
and agricultural purposes lime was manufactured locally, and there
are extensive remains of this early industrial activity at Shedden
Clough in the South Pennines.

By the 16th century lime was much in demand to make mortar for
building, leading to an increase in its extraction at Shedden. Old river
channels, or 'goits', and collection ponds show how water was diverted
from local streams. It was then released violently over the ground to
expose limestone fragments beneath the surface as the top layer of
earth was ripped away by the force of the water. Once extracted, the
limestone was burnt in kilns, many of whose remains lie scattered over
the area. The result, quicklime, was mixed with water to produce lime
putty, or with horsehair to form plaster. Farmers also added lime to
their soil to increase its productivity.

To see how some of the plaster based on Shedden lime was used, visit
the great hall at Towneley Hall; the elaborate plasterwork here is a
strong contrast to the eerie, pre-industrial revolution remains at Shedden. As was often the case, larger scale commercial kilns killed off the
smaller workings, but two of the newer, larger lime kilns have been
preserved alongside the canal in Burnley, to the rear of Sainsbury's.

Places of Interest in the Neighbourhood
  4. An Aladdin's Cave
11. Literary Corners
13. Steam Power
14. A Catholic Retreat
15. The Canal Town

13. Steam Power

Position: Burnley
O.S.Map: Landranger, Blackburn and Burnley, Sheet 103
Map Ref: 867 348
Access: The mill is in the Harle Syke north-east of the town centre. Accessible by car and regular bus service. It has recently undergone major refurbishment. For opening hours ring (01282) 412555. At the time of writing the mill was only open on weekdays, Tuesday to Friday and seasonally.

Queen Street Mill in Burnley is an authentic example of a still-working 19th century weaving shed, and is the country's last steam-powered textile mill. Built in the late 19th century, it closed in 1982 but has recently been renovated and reopened. 'Peace', the original 500 h.p. steam engine, still drives a shed of 308 Lancashire looms producing textiles for Queen Street Mill quality shirts.

Mill owners began to take increasing advantage of steam power as the 19th century progressed, exploiting its efficiency over water. Steam could power bigger mills and was less restrictive when choosing a site and so became widespread in both spinning and weaving. The introduction of Cartwright's steam-powered loom, though delayed by anti-mechanisation riots, helped steam's final victory over water power.

Places of Interest in the Neighbourhood
11. Literary Corners
14. A Catholic Retreat
15. The Canal Town
16. Impressive Entrances
17. The International Sun Dial

14. A Catholic Retreat

Position: Towneley Park, Burnley
O.S.Map: Landranger, Blackburn and Burnley, Sheet 103
Map Ref: 857 311
Access: On the south-eastern outskirts of Burnley, just off the A671.

Towneley Hall, the ancestral home of the resolutely Catholic Towneleys, contains a number of striking reminders of the strength of the family's faith and the hardships they had to endure from the time of Elizabeth I onwards. John Towneley, for example, suffered almost 25 years of continuous imprisonment until his release in 1593.

Foldys Cross lies behind the house at the top of Lime Tree Avenue (in fact a path). It was built in about 1520 and the Latin inscription around the base instructs you to pray for the soul of John Foldys,

Foldys Cross, Towneley Park, Burnley.

Chaplain. It stood intact in Burnley churchyard until 1789 when it was broken up, probably by a Puritan mob. The various pieces were carefully collected and resurrected at Towneley. It was moved to its present location in 1911, the Jubilee Year of Burnley Borough, and the Corporation had the cross restored. Some portions are original, and the base tier of seven steps is believed to be a copy of the original design.

Inside the Hall, the Whalley vestments are encased in glass. The two garments are extremely rare examples of a form of decorative medieval needlework known as Opus Anglicanum, and were originally worn by the priests administering High Mass. It is thought they were brought to Towneley Hall by Sir John Towneley (1473-1541) for safekeeping, after they had been rescued following the destruction of Whalley Abbey at the Dissolution.

The priests' hiding hole is one of several recorded as existing in the house. Its entrance is through a modern trap-door and reveals one of the largest priests' hiding places known, around eighteen by fifteen feet and tall enough to walk upright in. A clay and rush cover to the floor was intended to insulate the chamber in order to mute sound and stop detection. There are no written records of exactly who sheltered here, but it is presumed to be Elizabethan, and the subsequent pro-Royalist and pro-Jacobite sympathies of the Towneleys mean it may well have sheltered Cavaliers and Jacobites, as well as Catholic priests fleeing persecution.

The altarpiece in the Chapel is another masterpiece with its superb carving in Northern Rennaisance style. It was originally brought to the Hall in the late 18th century but was removed a century later, finally being repurchased in 1969. The upper part, dating from 1510-20, has panels depicting scenes from the Crucifixion. The lower section is probably late 17th century and depicts the Last Supper, the Virgin and St. Anne and the miracle of Manna from Heaven.

Places of Interest in the Neighbourhood
11. Literary Corners
13. Steam Power
15. The Canal Town
16. Impressive Entrances
17. The International Sun Dial

28

15. The Canal Town

Position: Burnley
O.S.Map: Landranger, Blackburn and Burnley, Sheet 103
Map Ref: 839 324
Access: The Weavers' Triangle is close to Burnley town centre, to the south-west of the Town Hall, just before meeting the A682.

Burnley is still dominated by the Leeds-Liverpool Canal running through its centre. It brought cheaper goods and a reliable water supply for mills. Most outstanding of all is the canal area known as the Weavers' Triangle. Here you will find the old toll house (now a visitor centre), fine warehouses and a stretch of 19th century mills, forming perhaps the best Victorian industrial landscape in the county. The exterior of the buildings has changed little but their use has altered dramatically. The oldest warehouse is now a public house, its original design clearly modelled on a barn. The nearby wooden slatted exten-

The Weavers' Triangle on the Leeds-Liverpool Canal, Burnley.

sion is an even more remarkable late 19th century construction, its canopy overhanging the canal and still housing some of the original winching gear. This was one of the main wharves on the Canal, storing flour, sugar, cotton, lime and malt. Other features include an incline for pulling out horses, rope marks on the stone work and a guide wheel for winding tow ropes around. Passing further down the canal decline rather than renovation has taken hold of the Victorian mills which still, however, maintain their original form. Look out for the unusual footbridge over the canal on this stretch.

The canal is at its most imposing as it passes along a 60 feet high embankment through the heart of the town, allowing spectacular views of the town centre and the surrounding hills of Pendle, Black Hameldon and Boulsworth.

Places of Interest in the Neighbourhood
11. Literary Corners
13. Steam Power
14. A Catholic Retreat
16. Impressive Entrances
17. The International Sun Dial

The gatehouse to Huntroyde Hall, Padiham.

16. Impressive Entrances

Position: The towns of Padiham and Gisburn
O.S.Map: Landranger, Blackburn and Burnley, Sheet 103
Map Ref: 786 342 and 828 488
Access: Arbory Lodge is just out of Padiham town centre on the A671, on Arbory Drive, on the right of the A671 just after the A678 to Clayton-le-Moors has split off to the left. The Gisburn lodges are at the southern entrance of Gisburn Park, near Gisburn village.

Local lords of the manor were often eager to make an impression on those entering their estates, sometimes erecting grand entrance lodges. At Padiham, an iron gateway and arch link two lodges, complete with fake battlements. The lodges and arch were built in about 1800 as an entrance to Huntroyde Hall, home of the Starkie family, who had acquired the estate when it was used for hunting in the Middle Ages. The lodge is now a private home, but the wrought iron gates are original.

Built around the same time but in a more ornate 'Gothick' style two symmetrical lodges guard the southern entrance to Gisburn Park. Both are two storey, though the exterior gives the impression of one tall storey. The tall pointed windows and pinnacles are typical of the Gothic revival of the late eighteenth century.

Places of Interest in the Neighbourhood
15. The Canal Town
25. A Fêted Son
55. A Viaduct in Praise of a Monastery

17. The International Sun Dial

Position: Nelson
O.S.Map: Landranger, Blackburn and Burnley, Sheet 103
Map Ref: 875 381
Access: Marsden Park is signed coming out of Nelson whilst following signs for Keighley (A6068).

In Marsden Park stands surely one of the most unusual sun dials in the world. It is icosahedral (twenty sided), and indicates the current time at such diverse places as Washington, Moscow, Jerusalem and Adam's Peak in Sri Lanka. It was made by an American master mason at the request of the then owner of Marsden Hall, R.T.R.Walton. Thanks to him Marsden Park is a veritable treasure trove; a mix of beautiful, fascinating and obscure features.

The Wishing Gate is found along a wooded pathway. A scrolled iron gateway is attached to a beautiful stone archway, each stone carved in different detail. Close to the Wishing Gate is a sunken garden, created by Walton for his two sisters and known as My Lady's Garden.

The small lake in the park was also created by Walton. Remains of unfinished, imitation open air Roman baths stand nearby, including arches, Fleur de Lys and shields. Throughout the grounds are numerous carved blocks of stone. Local tradition has it that they were the work of a former beggar in return for alms given to him by Walton. One work led to others, including a peacock and lions.

Walton died in 1845 and clearly had a place in the heart of the local community; his funeral procession was a mile in length. An 18th century extension to the hall has been demolished but the 16th century Tudor Hall has been renovated for use as a restaurant.

Places of Interest in the Neighbourhood
19. Turnpike Reminder
20. Nearer My God to Thee
21. The Prospect Tower without a Prospect
22. The Eye of Superstition

18.   The Valley of the Seven Bridges

Position: Wycoller (S. Pennines)
O.S.Map: Landranger; Blackburn and Burnley Sheet 103
Map Ref: 933 393
Access: There are 2 access roads to Wycoller, both with parking areas
(no parking in Wycoller). The first is off the A6068, east of Colne at
Laneshaw Bridge. The second is reached from Trawden town centre
off the B6250. A walk of a few hundred metres is necessary to reach the
curiosities.

The hamlet of Wycoller lies hidden to the outside world in Wycoller
Dean, or the Valley of the Seven Bridges, and houses antique bridges
and an ancient ruined hall.
   Perhaps most unusual of all is the Iron Age Clam Bridge, one of the
oldest bridges in the British Isles, really no more than a huge slab
of gritstone, seemingly finely balanced on supporting chunks of rock
either side of picturesque Wycoller Beck. Downstream, by the ruins of

The Iron Age Clam Bridge, Wycoller Beck.

Wycoller Hall, lie Clapper Bridge and an old well-worn 13th century packhorse bridge, one of its tiny arches endearingly irregular in shape. The former reflects the village's status in the 17th and 18th centuries as a thriving handloom weaving community, clapper being a general name for this early type of bridge - a name which may derive from the sound made by weavers' clogs.

Ironically it may have been decline, along with its isolated position, that has preserved Wycoller from the ravages of the twentieth century. Wycoller Hall fell into disuse after its owner, Henry Cunliffe, died in 1818, leaving considerable unpaid debts. The weaving community also deserted following the Industrial Revolution, leaving behind a virtual ghost village. It was only in the 1970's that private owners, together with Lancashire County Council, started to renovate properties. Today Wycoller is the centre of Wycoller Country Park and houses an information centre.

Places of Interest in the Neighbourhood
17. The International Sun Dial
20. Nearer My God to Thee

The old toll house, Barrowford.

19. Turnpike Reminder

Position: Barrowford
O.S.Map: Landranger, Blackburn and Burnley, Sheet 103
Map Ref: 864 404
Access: On the A682 in Barrowford, near the Pendle Heritage Centre, at the junction with the B6247.

Toll paying turnpike roads were the 18th century equivalent of our 'A' roads although wagons, livestock and people, not cars, would have been the traffic. Barrowford's toll house remains. It has been restored, even to the extent of recreating a toll board listing the traffic which might have used the turnpike, which originally ran from Nelson (then Marsden) to Long Preston. Wide-wheeled vehicles were charged less than narrow-wheeled ones of the same weight as it was thought wide wheels would help flatten the track surface rather than cut it up.

When this toll house was built in 1805 the system of turnpike roads was well established; by 1760 Preston and Burnley were linked to all the other major towns in the county. The roads were upgraded by specially created turnpike trusts, empowered by government to charge tolls, and their spread reflected the growth of textile production and population centres in the area. Coal was charged at a lower rate than other goods as many turnpike trustees were coal owners, and mail coaches and church-goers were usually exempt. Along with canals, turnpikes were a vital element in Lancashire's transport system before the coming of the railways, whose arrival in the 1840s spelt the end of the turnpike system. Barrowford toll house has been refurbished and is now used as a holiday cottage.

Places of Interest in the Neighbourhood
17. The International Sun Dial
20. Nearer My God to Thee
21. The Prospect Tower without a Prospect
22. The Eye of Superstition

20. Nearer My God to Thee

Position: Colne
O.S.Map: Landranger, Blackburn and Burnley, Sheet 103
Map Ref: 885 400
Access: From Market street, in the centre of Colne, head westwards
past St. Bartholomew's church onto Albert Road. The Wallace
Hartley Memorial is past the Municipal Hall near the War Memorial.

Outside of Colne few have heard of Wallace Hartley. Although he
died in 1912 his name is preserved here, in the form of a bronze bust.
A humble bank clerk in the town, he became a ship's bandmaster
for the Cunard Company, successfully entertaining the passengers on
80 trans-Atlantic crossings. In 1912 his career reached a new if ill-
fated summit, with his appointment as bandmaster on the *Titanic*,
then about to set sail on its maiden voyage. After the liner struck an
iceberg, Hartley summoned his band and began playing 'Nearer My
God to Thee' as the ship went down. 1,500 lives were lost that night,
Hartley amongst them. After his body arrived from Halifax, Nova
Scotia, some 40,000 people lined the streets for his funeral. Look out
for the belfry of the old Cloth Hall and one of the oldest gas lamps in
town, preserved near the bust.

Places of Interest in the Neighbourhood
17. The International Sun Dial
18. The Valley of the Seven Bridges
19. Turnpike Reminder
21. The Prospect Tower without a Prospect

The memorial to Wallace Hartley, Colne.

WALLACE
HARTLEY

BANDMASTER OF
THE R.M.S TITANIC
WHO PERISHED IN
THE FOUNDERING
OF THAT VESSEL
APRIL 15ᵗʰ, 1912.

ERECTED BY VOLUNTARY
CONTRIBUTIONS TO COM-
MEMORATE THE HEROISM
OF A NATIVE OF THIS
TOWN

21. The Prospect Tower without a Prospect

Position: Near Blacko hamlet, north of Barrowford
O.S.Map: Landranger, Blackburn and Burnley, Sheet 103
Map Ref: 859 422
Access: The nearest public access is the public footpath to the east of the tower, accessible from the south.

Blacko Tower, also known as Stansfield Tower, was built in 1890 to give its builder, local grocer John Stansfield, a view over Ribblesdale. Unfortunately, the circular tower turned out to be too short to give the desired prospect, but it does provide fine views over Pendle Hill, Nelson, Colne and the South Pennines! The inscription PS 127 IV on the tower's datestone refers to a Psalm. In 1964 the building was anonymously whitewashed under cover of darkness. Nobody seems to know why!

Places of Interest in the Neighbourhood
19. Turnpike Reminder
20. Nearer My God to Thee
22. The Eye of Superstition

Blacko Tower, Blacko.

22. The Eye of Superstition

Position: Newchurch in Pendle
O.S.Map: Landranger; Blackburn and Burnley, Sheet 103
Map Ref: 824 394
Access: Newchurch in Pendle is south-east of Pendle Hill, west of
Barrowford and Nelson.

Strolling round the graveyard at Newchurch in Pendle you may be
tempted to think the pretty, neatly proportioned 18th century church
shows little out of the ordinary. However, close inspection of the
masonry beneath the clock on the tower reveals a strange carved oval
with a circle at its centre. Curiously named the 'Eye of God' by locals,
its supposed function is to ward off evil but there is no written record
of its significance and its true purpose must be lost to the passage of
time.

A further enigmatic feature is the grave marked with skull and
crossbones bearing the name 'Nutter'. Conjectures that this is the
grave of one of the Pendle Witches, Alice Nutter, are surely wrong,
conveniently ignoring the fact that witches were never buried in consecrated ground. The real legacy of the Pendle Witches still lingers in
numerous places throughout Lancashire. The powerful mix of a king
fearful of witchcraft (James I) and the feuding of the Demdike and
Chattox family clans in the Pendle area ended in 1612 with the hanging
of several 'witches' after their imprisonment at Lancaster Castle.
During the trial it was testified that Mother Chattox took four teeth
and three scalps from bodies in Newchurch churchyard. The Demdike
clan lived at Malkin Tower whose possible location was Malkin Tower
Farm (map ref: 864 421), although this is hotly disputed. In contrast to
the terror-inspiring old hags, Demdike and Chattox, Alice Nutter was
a highly respected lady and her silent acquiescence to her hanging is a
mystery. One theory is that, as a staunch Catholic, she kept quiet
about her own activities to protect other Catholics at a time when
Catholic services were illegal. Her house at Roughlee still stands today
(map ref: 845 404).

Places of Interest in the Neighbourhood
19. Turnpike Reminder
21. The Prospect Tower without a Prospect

23. A Rare Relic of Norman Agriculture

Position: Standen Hey Farm, 2-3 kilometres south of Clitheroe
O.S.Map: Landranger, Blackburn and Burnley, Sheet 103
Map Ref: 734 394
Access: Standen Hey Farm drive is a public footpath off the A671 near Limehouse Farm.

This beautiful multi-arched barn stands amidst an unremarkable group of farmhouses which only serve to emphasise its antiquity. Although sadly decayed, the arches that allowed several carts to simultaneously load up with corn are well preserved. The building is the oldest of its kind in Lancashire.

Standen Hey served as a collection and distribution point for corn. There were a number of barns established here after the De Lacy family founded a corn mill between Henthorn and Siddows. The mill passed into the hands of the crown and became known as King's Mill. The crown enjoyed high rents from the mill, whose miller enjoyed a monopoly by working the only corn mill on crown lands - a cosy arrangement which lasted until early in the 19th century.

Places of Interest in the Neighbourhood
55. A Viaduct in Praise of a Monastery
56. Immortalised in Alabaster

The old barn at Standen Hey Farm, near Clitheroe.

24. In Roman Footsteps

Position: Quiet countryside between Whalley and Great Mitton
O.S.Map: Landranger, Blackburn and Burnley, Sheet 103
Map Ref: 728 386
Access: Footpath signed from the B6246, about one and a half kilometres south of Great Mitton. Hardhill Cross is then less than a kilometre on the footpath. Boots are essential as the ground can be very marshy. Standen Hey barn is further on.

Some agility is required crossing the stepping stones over a brook on the way to this ancient cross base. After a while your path becomes obvious, near the left hand side of a huge field. The course of the Roman road is difficult to decipher, but in places what is probably the original surface emerges in the form of cobbles. Carrying on in a straight line on the course of this road you soon come upon a massive, square stone with an impressive square socket hewn out of the middle.

Hardhill Cross and the Roman road near Great Mitton.

41

Known as Hardhill Cross, it is now recognised as the socket base for a Roman milestone. The course of the road is marked on the Landranger map and can be seen extending westwards to Ribchester and beyond and roughly north-eastwards, passing south of Clitheroe and north of Downham village. At the latter spot the cobbles are also visible. Many legionnaires must have trodden the course of the road linking what are today the settlements of Ribchester and Ilkley, and a large stone by Downham Hall entrance is said to mark the burial site of two who died during a time of conflict with the local Brigantine tribes.

The Romans also erected a bridge over a brook near Hardhill Cross consisting of two large stone slabs. Unfortunately the bridge and adjoining Roman road surface have been all but destroyed by the effects of motorcycle scrambles, making public awareness of the value of what remains here all the more important.

Places of Interest in the Neighbourhood
55. A Viaduct in Praise of a Monastery
56. Immortalised in Alabaster

The monument to John Mercer, Great Harwood.

25. A Fêted Son

Position: Great Harwood, north of Blackburn
O.S.Map: Landranger, Blackburn and Burnley, Sheet 103
Map Ref: 733 322
Access: The Mercer monument is in the centre of Great Harwood market square.

The progress of cotton manufacture in Lancashire from cottage industry to 'King Cotton' depended upon technological advances, most of which were the products of fertile Lancastrian minds with a strong practical bent. By the 19th century the industry had become mechanised to a large degree and moved into huge mills employing thousands of men, women and children.

It was left to men like John Mercer, Great Harwood's most famous son, to introduce sophisticated processes into the industry to keep it at the forefront of the world market. Born in Great Harwood in 1791, he became an industrial chemist and invented the 'mercerisation' technique which put a glossy sheen onto manufactured cotton, making it more marketable. In 1903 the proud residents of Great Harwood erected a clocktower monument to him that now stands in the centre of the market square.

Whilst in Great Harwood seek out Mautholme, a Grade I listed manor house (map ref: 753 338).

Places of Interest in the Neighbourhood

26. 'Fairy Caves' of Early Industry

Position: Oswaldtwistle, near Accrington
O.S.Map: Landranger, Blackburn and Burnley, Sheet 103
Map Ref: 736 285
Access: Just off the A679 running north of Oswaldtwistle, wedged between the Leeds-Liverpool Canal and the railway line. Cross over the canal by the bridge at map ref: 734 284.

In the mid-19th century Lancashire was still at the forefront of international industry. Most important of all was cotton, but deep mining of coal in the east of the county also played a part. Like cotton, the coal industry collapsed and the only real reminder of it in this area today are the 'beehive' coke ovens or 'fairy caves', a name springing from their use by local children as playgrounds.

Three banks of these curious conical, brick constructions, where coal was burnt with a minimum of air to produce coke, remain. The ovens still reveal tunnel flues and a lining of refractory bricks, made of a local material to withstand the heat. The Leeds-Liverpool Canal was specially diverted to carry the products of the mines, and the coke was loaded at a nearby dock to be transported on to Preston and Lancaster.

Places of Interest in the Neighbourhood

The remains of the old coke ovens north of Oswaldtwistle.

27. The Scaled-Down Cathedral

Position: Blackburn
O.S.Map: Landranger, Blackburn and Burnley, Sheet 103
Map Ref: 681 279
Access: At the heart of Blackburn town centre. Plenty of parking and train access.

Blackburn Cathedral was formerly St. Mary's Church and today represents a fascinating blend of tradition and modernity, a blend that came about partly by accident. It is really a church of two parts; the older part, which now functions as the nave, was built largely in 1831

The spire and tower of Blackburn Cathedral.

after a fire had destroyed much of the 1826 base. In 1926 Blackburn became a diocese and in keeping with its status St. Mary's Church became Blackburn Cathedral.

Initial designs for expansion were grandiose, envisaging a new, massive central tower crowning a large new extension. Work began enthusiastically in 1938, only to be interrupted by the outbreak of the Second World War. Building was suspended, and post-1945 austerity eventually forced a complete reappraisal of the plans. The base of the new extension was already established at the crossing of the nave and transept, and included vestries, meeting rooms and a library. The greatest change was the design for the new tower, and a scaled-down but perhaps more striking tower was finally built. Its glazed octagon of reinforced concrete provides a solid yet elegant base for the needle-like tower. Together they make a perfect, almost futuristic complement to the traditional western tower. Inside are numerous works of art; in particular look out for 'Christ the Worker', a giant sculpture by John Hayward.

Places of Interest in the Neighbourhood
26. 'Fairy Caves' of Early Industry
28. What a Relief!
29. The Incomplete Exchange
31. Venice Visits Darwen
32. Some Splendid Conveniences

28. What a Relief!

Position: Blackburn
O.S.Map: Landranger, Blackburn and Burnley, Sheet 103
Map Ref: Free Library and Museum 683 283. Technical School nearby
on Blakey Moor college site
Access: Plenty of town centre parking and central train station.

Seven fascinating relief panels decorate the outside of Blackburn Free
Library and Museum. Each was paid for by local dignitaries and
represents a different theme: Iron Founding, Art, Literature, Science,
Agriculture, Textiles and Commerce. The main building was built in
the 1870s but the panels, by the London sculptor C.W.Seale, were
added in the 1890s when the building was extended. The museum
houses a number of unusual collections, including a gallery dedicated
to Muslim and Hindu culture and the Hart collection of illuminated
manuscripts, early printed books and coins.

The superb façade of the nearby Technical School building also
contains exquisite relief carvings and demonstrates a lavish French
Renaissance style. It celebrates Queen Victoria's 1887 Golden Jubilee
and was opened in 1891.

Places of Interest in the Neighbourhood
26. 'Fairy Caves' of Early Industry
27. The Scaled-Down Cathedral
29. The Incomplete Exchange
31. Venice Visits Darwen
32. Some Splendid Conveniences

*'Iron Founding', one of the reliefs on the outside of Blackburn Free
Library and Museum.*

29. The Incomplete Exchange

Position: Blackburn
O.S.Map: Landranger, Blackburn and Burnley, Sheet 103
Map Ref: 682 282
Access: Plenty of town centre parking and central train station.

In the mid-19th century Blackburn was booming and the town's cotton-based wealth financed a series of exotic buildings, including a Town Hall and new market house. The Blackburn Cotton Exchange was designed in the 14th century gothic style and the original plan was for a tower flanked by two long wings. Its foundation stone was laid in 1860, the decade that unfortunately saw the so-called 'cotton famine', a shortage of raw cotton caused by the blockade of the southern American cotton growing states during the Civil War. As a result the mill owners' company, formed specifically to build the exchange, ran short of funds and only the central tower and one wing were built. The resulting room measured an impressive 140 feet by 53 feet. The interior of the building largely disappeared and it now houses a cinema and restaurant, though the magnificent exterior remains intact.

Places of Interest in the Neighbourhood
26. 'Fairy Caves' of Early Industry
27. The Scaled-Down Cathedral
28. What a Relief!
31. Venice Visits Darwen
32. Some Splendid Conveniences

The Cotton Exchange, Blackburn.

30. A Penny a Pot

Position: Haslingden
O.S.Map: Landranger, Blackburn and Burnley, Sheet 103
Map Ref: 778 215
Access: From the A56 Haslingden by-pass. For opening times contact (01706) 226459.

Helmshore Textile Museums consist of two mill buildings. Higher Mill dates from 1789, thus making it probably the oldest mill in Lancashire, and today provides the unique sight of a pair of 'fulling' hammers in action. Woollen cloth was 'fulled' by being continually soaked and then pounded with huge hammers. The 18 feet waterwheel produced the tremendous force necessary to drive the massive hammers, which in turn compressed the woven woollen textile, tightening the weave. One advantage of working at the mill might have been the offer of 'a penny a pot' for your urine, originally used as a cleansing agent in the fulling process! The hammers' thirty nine beats per minute, producing only a thirty yard piece of cloth a day, was an improvement on trampling the cloth to help full it.

Places of Interest in the Neighbourhood
  3. The Wet Tower
  5. Britain's Last Temperance Bar
  6. A Cottage with a Purpose
40. Two Lonely Monuments

31. Venice Visits Darwen

Position: Darwen
O.S.Map: Landranger, Blackburn and Burnley, Sheet 103
Map Ref: 694 218
Access: The tower is a notable landmark visible from some distance away. Approach on the A666 heading south out of Darwen.

Lancashire's industrial heartland might be the last place you expect to see a replica of the bell tower in St. Mark's Square in Venice, but India Mill boasts just such a structure. At 300 ft tall it is clearly modelled on

India Mill, Darwen.

this masterpiece of Venetian architecture. Its iron cap weighs around forty tons and there are wide platforms near the summit. It was started in 1867, and took fourteen years to build out of Cadshaw stone and locally hand-made bricks at a cost of £12,000. It is ironic that the Venetian original fell down in 1902 and was replaced by a replica! The exterior styling of the India Mill factory itself also shows the increasing trend of the mid-19th century for mill-owners and designers to put considerable thought into the styling of their factories.

On display near the front of the mill on the main Blackburn road is a large 'cross-compound' type engine used to power looms, and a wallpaper machine stands close by.

Places of Interest in the Neighbourhood
32. Some Splendid Conveniences
33. Tocca's Valley
34. Pagan or Catholic Spring?
35. A Tower with a Double Purpose

The tram shelters in Darwen.

32. Some Splendid Conveniences

Position: Darwen
O.S.Map: Landranger, Blackburn and Burnley, Sheet 103
Map Ref: 692 223
Access: Visible as you pass through the town centre, next to the main A666.

At first glance it is difficult to guess the purpose of the two ornate, domed buildings next to the main road in Darwen. They are in fact tram shelters, but also incorporate 'his' and 'hers'. They were built in 1902 and originally contained subterranean toilets with waiting rooms above, and a parcel room behind the 'gents'. They are currently disused, although their exteriors, including copper domes and wrought ironwork, are generally in a good state of repair.

Darwen's steam tramway system began operating in 1888, superseding horse-bus routes, and was electrified in 1900. Some trams upper decks were covered, allegedly only on routes to 'posh' areas such as Hoddlesden. Darwen's last tram ran in 1946, with souvenir tickets being handed out by the Mayor and Mayoress.

Places of Interest in the Neighbourhood
31. Venice Visits Darwen
33. Tocca's Valley
34. Pagan or Catholic Spring?
35. A Tower with a Double Purpose

33. Tocca's Valley

Position: Tockholes, west of Darwen
O.S.Map: Landranger, Blackburn and Burnley, Sheet 103
Map Ref: 659 235
Access: This small village is between Blackburn and Bolton, on a minor road between the A675 and A666.

Tockholes is derived from 'Tocca's Valley', an old Saxon name dating back to the 8th century. Even today the village feels somewhat isolated from the 20th century and is still home to a variety of curiosities.

Standing in the churchyard is the old schoolhouse, dating from around 1900-1910, which has an unusual outdoor pulpit and mullioned windows. The pulpit replaces an earlier wooden one from Mellor church. The most unusual grave here is that of John Osbaldeston, the inventor of the weft fork, a device for stopping a loom should a thread break. Osbaldeston told some friends of his invention during

The outdoor pulpit at the old schoolhouse, Tockholes.

a drinking session, who in turn capitalised on his ingenuity and gained the wealth that was rightly his. He wrote his own epitaph but no one had the courage to inscribe it on his memorial:

Here Lies
John Osbaldeston
a Humble Inventor who raised many to Wealth and Fortune
but Himself lived in Poverty and Died in Obscurity
a Dupe of False Friends and the
Victim of Misplaced Confidence

His grave is marked by the tall, conically-pointed column behind the present wooden church.

Beware of the tale on the so-called 'ancient tocha's stone', near the front of the church. Despite the inscription, a local openly admitted it was carved some decades ago by another resident! The withered looking top may, however, be the remnants of a Saxon preaching cross.

To the east of the church, just up the lane, is an old well with an inscribed stone arch telling us it is Norman and was removed from Gerstane Hall before its demolition and placed here in 1910.

Places of Interest in the Neighbourhood
31. Venice Visits Darwen
32. Some Splendid Conveniences
34. Pagan or Catholic Spring?
35. A Tower with a Double Purpose

34. Pagan or Catholic Spring?

Position: On the west side of Darwen Hill near the Tockholes Road
O.S.Map: Landranger, Blackburn and Burnley, Sheet 103
Map Ref: 661 204
Access: A track leads from the Tockholes road to Hollinshead Hall ruins. Parking on the same road about 1 kilometre to the north, before reaching the hamlet of Ryal Fold (information centre here).

Amidst the gardens of the ruined Hollinshead Hall lies a well-preserved outbuilding housing a stone carved lion's head that emits a small spring of water. The spring falls into a central channel, surrounded by cisterns and benches on either side. This fascinating building is Hollinshead Well, whose original purpose is hotly debated.

Its origin seems likely to be ancient. The vaulting inside may be from the 15th century whilst the covering is from the 18th. Some believe it to be of pagan origin as it reportedly contains the water of five separate springs, signalling the presence of the water-goddess. More recently it seems to have been used as a Catholic baptistery, with the two cisterns perhaps being used for male and female baptisms. Records show medieval pilgrims visited the well to try and cure ophthalmic complaints.

Places of Interest in the Neighbourhood
Hollinshead Well, in the gardens of Hollinshead Hall.

35. A Tower with a Double Purpose

Position: West of Darwen
O.S.Map: Landranger, Blackburn and Burnley, Sheet 103
Map Ref: 679 216
Access: There are a number of footpath approaches to the tower
across moorland.

Described as the finest prospect tower in Lancashire, Darwen Tower
was built to celebrate the 1897 Diamond Jubilee of Queen Victoria. It
could also be said to commemorate a second event, though unlike the
Jubilee this is not recorded anywhere on the tower. An anonymous

Darwen Tower.

letter to the *Darwen News* first suggested the tower, stating that not only would it be a fitting tribute to the Queen but also to a legal victory allowing local people access to the moor. This was achieved in 1896 after the 'Freedom Movement', a group of locals, took the lord of the manor to the High Court in London and won the right to wander on the moor.

Much of its structure was blown away by severe gales in 1947. It seemed condemned to rot away until it was re-opened in 1972 following a programme of restoration. There is a viewing platform halfway up and a viewing turret crowns the tower. The viewfinder on top boasts such distant landmarks as Snowdon and the Isle of Man though you will need an exceptionally clear day to see them, but it still gives excellent views and Blackpool Tower and Pendle Beacon can usually be seen.

Places of Interest in the Neighbourhood
31. Venice Visits Darwen
32. Some Splendid Conveniences
33. Tocca's Valley
34. Pagan or Catholic Spring?

36.   Stone and Bronze Age Burials

Position: The Pikestones are found on Anglezarke Moor, to the north of Horwich
O.S.Map: Landranger, Preston and Blackpool, Sheet 102
Map Ref: 626 172
Access: Via a footpath north-west of the Lead Mines Clough area and alongside a plantation. (Note the footpath is concessionary and not marked on maps. The Pikestones are marked 'chambered long cairn'.) Walking boots are essential and careful navigation is required.

The remains of a megalithic tomb lie nearly 300 metres high on the side of Hurst Hill. The tomb has been badly robbed but two stones remain standing at its eastern end, giving you some idea of what this fourteen feet long tomb must have originally looked like. It is thought to be Neolithic, or about 7,000 years old, and was probably abandoned following deforestation by Neolithic man and a climate change which made the area more inhospitable.

Discovered only a century ago, a Bronze Age burial circle near Bleasdale is around 3,000 years old (map ref: 577 460). It is reachable on foot only, from the track north of Bleasdale. Access is by arrangement with Vicarage Farm opposite the track leading to the circle. A 150 feet diameter ditch encircles the site where remains of two cremations were found in burial urns.

Places of Interest in the Neighbourhood
37. The Fanciful Creations of a Public-Spirited Industrialist
38. Defensive Tower or Industrialist's Fancy?
39. Legacies of the Steam Age

37. The Fanciful Creations of a Public-Spirited Industrialist

Position: Just outside Horwich, near Bolton
O.S.Map: Landranger, Manchester, Sheet 109
Map Ref: Lever Park covers extensive grounds north-west of a parking ground at 634 128
Access: Leaving Horwich in a north-westerly direction on the A673 turn onto Lever Park Road just after a roundabout. This road then runs through the centre of the park, giving you access to the four main car parks.

Lever Park was at one time a weekend retreat of one of Bolton's most successful sons, William Hesketh Lever, later to become Lord Leverhulme. A humble grocer's son, Lever founded the Lever Brothers empire, based on soap, which later became Unilever, in the process acquiring a reputation as a successful businessman and a leading philanthropist. In 1900 he purchased what is today Lever Park, creating a private weekend residence whose landscaped gardens were full of small, idiosyncratic architectural gems.

Today the best preserved feature, the Pigeon Tower, lies atop a hill, a tall thin surreal edifice. Built in 1910 by one of Lever's main architects, T.H. Mawson, it consists of three storeys. It is said Lady Lever used the top one as a sewing room, keeping ornamental pigeons in the lower two (for illustration see frontispiece).

The best way to approach the Pigeon Tower is along the Terraced Gardens Trail, beginning at the car park by Rivington Hall. Although many of Lever's creations can still be seen, some are in a sorry state and others have been demolished altogether. The trail climbs through a series of steep terraces above a beautiful garden shelter of which there are many more. An army of gardeners was employed to plant the various trees and shrubs and to construct an artificial ravine, housing waterfalls, pools and a bridge. Further climbing reveals perhaps the saddest sight in the grounds; Mawson's once elegant Japanese Gardens have lost their pagodas and lanterns and are now overgrown. Further up the slope lie the sites of Lever's main residence, his circular ballroom and the Great Lawn.

Reaching the Pigeon Tower you can extend the visit to Pike Tower. This square tower squats on a magnificent 1,200 feet high viewpoint; on a clear day the Welsh mountains, the Isle of Man and the Cumbrian

One of the stone garden shelters at Lever Park.

fells are all visible. Bought as part of the Lever estate, the tower was nearly demolished, and owes its survival to public protest. Descending the trail look out for the swimming pool beneath the Pigeon Tower and the extraordinary Seven Arches Bridge, designed by Lever himself. The Rotary Club building in the car park is in fact a converted barn, as is the Information Centre at the bottom of Hall Drive, with parts of the structures dating from Saxon times.

On the banks of Lower Rivington Reservoir lies a replica of Liverpool Castle built by Lever between 1912 and 1925, and intended to recreate the ruined castle just prior to its demolition in 1725.

Places of Interest in the Neighbourhood
36. Stone and Bronze Age Burials
38. Defensive Tower or Industrialist's Fancy?
39. Legacies of the Steam Age

38. Defensive Tower or Industrialist's Fancy?

Position: Near Bolton
O.S.Map: Landranger, Manchester, Sheet 109
Map Ref: 731 153
Access: Heading north out of Bolton, Turton Tower is 2-3 kilometres out of Bromley Cross. Open to the public (closed December and January). For admission details contact (01204) 852203.

Turton Tower has been a residence for a wide variety of inhabitants throughout the ages and has accordingly changed its purpose and style radically, as reflected in the present-day building. Additions over the centuries have produced an unusual architectural mix.

There was probably a defensive tower here as early as the 12th century but the dominating stone pele tower you see today was built in about 1420. The next major phase of additions came in the 16th century when cruck-framed farmhouses were built next to the tower, which was itself enlarged. During the Civil War the house was owned by the treasurer of the Roundheads and, after being occupied by a succession of tenant farmers, it passed in 1835 to James Kay, a local 'cotton king', who restored the interior in the lavish Victorian style apparent in the oak panelling and plaster ceilings. All this work has produced a pleasing mix of Norman, Tudor, Stuart and Victorian styles! The tower is set in attractive countryside and contains a museum and tea room.

Places of Interest in the Neighbourhood
36. Stone and Bronze Age Burials
37. The Fanciful Creations of a Public-Spirited Industrialist
39. Legacies of the Steam Age
40. Two Lonely Monuments

Turton Tower, near Bolton.

39. Legacies of the Steam Age

Position: Near Turton Bottoms village, north of Bolton
O.S.Map: Landranger, Manchester, sheet 109
Map Ref: 729 152
Access: A public footpath leads over the bridge. From the B6391 follow
the main track past Turton Tower itself and continue onto the bridge.

The incised nature of Pennine scenery in East Lancashire meant some
spectacular viaducts and tunnels were built as the railways expanded.
We start, however, with the small scale but delightful little bridge near
Turton Tower. The owner of the house, James Kay, insisted it was built
in keeping with his residence, hence its castellated turrets and mock
medieval, cross shaped apertures. It provided access to estate grounds
beyond the railway and even had a staircase and seat in one of the
turrets. The single track over which the bridge passes is still in use today
as the Bolton to Blackburn line. After Turton Tower bridge the line
heads through a dramatic cutting before plunging into the 2,000 yard
Sough Tunnel.

The viaduct at Healey Dell (map ref: 880 160) is the tallest and visually
most spectacular of all Lancashire viaducts. It rises more than 100 feet
above the Sprodden gorge. It originally carried the line between Rochdale and Bacup, but the last train ran across it in 1967. It is now a
walking trail at the heart of Healey Dell Nature Reserve. Within easy
walking distance of the viaduct a beautiful gorge-side walk passes the
remains of several mills that were once tucked into the narrow gorge.

The problems posed by geography for the East Lancashire Railway
between Rawtenstall and Bacup were equally great. The Irwell Gorge,
known locally as 'The Glen', was too narrow to house the track and
the road existing prior to the railway had to be chiselled out in the
form of a rock ledge. The resulting Newchurch Tunnels of 1852 (map
ref: 838 216), though now bricked-up and not as visually spectacular as
Healey Dell, were an equally impressive feat of railway engineering. At
the time this was the only feasible route to Bacup; the Rochdale-Bacup
railway arrived only in the 1880s, after clawing its way over a 962 feet
summit, the highest point of the railway system in the central Pennines. The tunnel sections between Waterfoot and Stacksteads on the
A681 were known as Newchurch Tunnels, and were 162 and 290 yards
long respectively. A third tunnel was constructed twelve yards to the
south for a further line due to increased traffic. It required dynamiting
through 592 yards of solid rock and became known as 'the thrutch' to

the navvies who worked on it. A dictionary definition of this old Lancashire word might be something like 'to strain to the utmost of your ability'!

Places of Interest in the Neighbourhood
36. Stone and Bronze Age Burials
37. The Fanciful Creations of a Public-Spirited Industrialist
38. Defensive Tower or Industrialist's Fancy?
40. Two Lonely Monuments

The bridge over the railway near Turton Tower.

40. Two Lonely Monuments

Position: Near Bull Hill, south of Haslingden and Helmshore
O.S.Map: Landranger, Manchester, Sheet 109 (Blackburn and
Burnley, Sheet 103 also useful to show footpath access)
Map Ref: 775 193 (Ellen Strange Monument) and 773 182 (Pilgrims'
Cross)
Access: On foot from Sunnybank Road at the southern end of
Helmshore. A Ministry of Defence firing range is close to the
monuments, so watch out for red flags.

Much of the ground covered in reaching these two monuments is part
of the old Pilgrims' Way used on the trek to Whalley Abbey in
medieval times. On your ascent up Stake Lane, a track that can
become boggy, look out for Robin Hood's Well, a small spring the
pilgrims may have drunk from.
  The first monument, a cairn and memorial stone is reached shortly
after this, having emerged onto the open moorland. The stone bears
the initials E.S. which stand for Ellen Strange, a girl reputedly mur-
dered on this spot in 1735. She had been visiting Haslingden Fair with
her sweetheart and disappeared on the way home, and her sweetheart
was tried and hanged for her murder. More modern research appears
to contradict this tale. It seems Ellen Strange was a poor, married
woman, and although suspicion fell on her husband he was later ac-
quitted. You can pick out the faint form of a girl and other figures on
the monument.
  Continuing on the path you approach the stubby, square Pilgrims'
Cross monument. Unfortunately the impressive cross, marking the
pilgrims route to Whalley, was removed by vandals, in 1901. The
informative plaque was placed here by the Vicar of Holcombe and
gives a brief history of the cross, from its earliest known existence in
the 12th century to its enigmatic disappearance. Whalley Abbey itself
is featured in curiosity 55.

Places of Interest in the Neighbourhood
  3. The Wet Tower
 30. A Penny a Pot
 37. The Fanciful Creations of a Public-Spirited Industrialist
 38. Defensive Tower or Industrialist's Fancy?

41. Shove-ha'penny, Elizabethan Style

Position: Astley Hall, Chorley
O.S.Map: Landranger, Liverpool, Sheet 108. Town centre map useful
Map Ref: 574 183
Access: Near the Tourist Information Centre in Chorley town centre.
Free admission.

In the early 17th century long gallery of Astley Hall is a twenty-four
feet long table, resting on twenty turned legs with intricate carvings
around the edge. It may appear at first glance to be a great banqueting
table but an unusual game was also played on it. Sizeable flat weights
were 'shoved' the length of the table, presumably to within as small a
distance as possible of the far end. There are also marked lines on the
table; probably for measuring the length of a 'shove', but the exact
rules of the game are not known any longer. It was, in effect a giant
Elizabethan version of shove-ha'penny!

Astley Hall was donated to the people of Chorley in 1922 and is
now the town Museum. Much of the original Elizabethan construction remains. After a look round the museum there is also a cafe and
parkland to be enjoyed. For further details contact the museum on
(01257) 262166.

Places of Interest in the Neighbourhood
36. Stone and Bronze Age Burials
37. The Fanciful Creations of a Public-Spirited Industrialist
48. Lancashire's Biggest Draught Excluder

The Parbold Bottle monument, Parbold.

42. A Democratic Monument

Position: Near Parbold village, north of Skelmersdale
O.S.Map: Landranger, Liverpool, Sheet 108
Map Ref: 508 105
Access: Take the A5209 eastwards from Parbold. About a kilometre out of Parbold a small track leads down the side of a quarry to Parbold Bottle.

Although the scale of Parbold Bottle monument is not impressive, its purpose is unusual. Constructed of local gritstone, it resembles an antique rather than a modern bottle. It commands excellent views over the coastal plain and Douglas Valley, and landmarks such as Blackpool Tower are also visible.

It was constructed to commemorate the 1832 Reform Act, and it is strange to think that this secluded monument celebrates some of the most tumultuous events in British history. In the early 1830s there was much popular protest in favour of greater voting rights. A Tory government backed by a conservative House of Lords resisted several times, but increasingly violent protest forced the King to create extra, sympathetic peers in order for the Reform Bill to proceed through the Lords. As a result the right to vote was extended to a significant proportion of the 'middle' classes.

Places of Interest in the Neighbourhood
43. The Last of the Beacons
44. A Watery Landmark

43. The Last of the Beacons

Position: Just north of Skelmersdale
O.S.Map: Landranger, Liverpool, Sheet 108
Map Ref: 501 079
Access: A minor road north east of Skelmersdale runs through Beacon Country Park. There is a parking ground near the beacon and also good footpath access for those wanting to walk from the pretty Douglas Valley to the north.

Beacons were traditionally lit to warn of imminent national danger, such as the Spanish Armada. By the time of the Napoleonic wars in the late 18th century many such sites had fallen into disrepair, but the fear of invasion meant that many were made again. Some were manned, and small barracks were built to house the necessary soldiers.

Ashurst's Beacon, built in 1798 by Lord Skelmersdale on Ashurst's Hill, may have been constructed for just such a reason. Its doors and windows are now blocked up and it is a local landmark at the centre of a country park. Other Lancashire beacon sites include nearby Billinge Hill (whose building's pyramidal top has been lost) and Pendle Hill, where no such building exists.

Places of Interest in the Neighbourhood
42. A Democratic Monument
44. A Watery Landmark

Ashurst's Beacon, near Skelmersdale.

Tower Hill water tower, near Ormskirk.

44. A Watery Landmark

Position: East of Ormskirk
O.S.Map: Landranger, Liverpool, Sheet 108
Map Ref: 424 085
Access: Leaving Ormskirk on the A577 towards Skelmersdale turn left by the hospital. Tower Hill water tower is less than half a kilometre down the road and is easily visible when you approach it.

The remains of this distinctive water tower are thought to be the oldest surviving example in the country. The tower was built in the 1850s for Ormskirk Local Board of Health. Originally a tank sat at a height of 55 feet above two tall Romanesque arches. A spiral staircase in the central pier led to an upper chamber where windows were located between the stones projecting from beneath the tank and acting as supports. Today all that remains are the huge arched supports and the tank base with unusual lion carvings at the corners.

The water tower at Tower Hill is a well-known local landmark, but it is also a reminder of an age when Ormskirk's water supply came from wells and ditches, many of which were contaminated. A national outbreak of cholera in 1847 produced the 1848 Public Health Act and a clean, pressurised system of water was designed for Ormskirk. Prior to the act a government inspector had counted 117 people waiting to use a single pump! There were originally four towers in the system, which continued in use until the mid 1970s when they were demolished and their role taken by the newly-constructed, giant 'flying saucer' tower at Scarth Hill, visible for miles around.

Places of Interest in the Neighbourhood
42. A Democratic Monument
43. The Last of the Beacons

45. A Wooden Church

Position: Altcar, near Formby
O.S.Map: Landranger, Liverpool, Sheet 108
Map Ref: 319 066
Access: Visible from the B5195, a couple of kilometres outside Formby.

The Church of St. Michael's in Great Altcar resembles a cross between a church and a timber-framed house, and is the only timber-framed church in Lancashire. The influence of the Chester architect who designed it is clear, as the black timber frame and white panelling resemble many of the houses in Chester. This 1879 architectural experiment typifies the way in which the age was struggling to find a style which it could call its own; there are more 'mock' styles from the Victorian period than any other. Inside, the church combines a marriage between a place of worship and a barn, with timber posts supporting the rafters.

Places of Interest in the Neighbourhood
46. The Boulevard where East Meets West

The Church of St. Michael's, Great Altcar.

46. The Boulevard where East Meets West

Position: Southport
O.S.Map: Landranger, Liverpool, Sheet 108
Map Ref: 336 174 and around
Access: Lord Street is at the heart of Southport town centre.

Lord Street, at the centre of elegant Southport, has been described as one of the most attractive boulevards in the whole of Europe. Its huge range of architectural styles blend together to produce a sophisticated and fascinating atmosphere. Perhaps most unusual is the eastern influence seen in the pointed horseshoe windows of the 'Muslim Buildings' between numbers 319 and 325. Some of the other 'mock' styles represented are; Italian Renaissance (National Westminster Bank), Elizabethan and Early English Gothic (Albany Buildings) and Roman Corinthian (Midland Bank) as well as ornate canopies and arcades with friezes, mouldings and stained glass windows. The civic buildings are also of note; the beautiful white Town Hall was designed in the classical style by local architect Thomas Withnell. Nearby is one of the country's most impressive war memorials, consisting of an obelisk in the centre of two long colonnades inside which are listed numerous campaigns.

This incredible mix of architecture has been retained by several factors. At its foundation Southport was aimed at the 'well-to-do', initially as a bathing resort then a residential town. William Sutton opened the first summer lodging house in 1792, shortly afterwards founding the South Port Hotel, which in turn gave the town its name. Initial leases stipulated that buildings could not be of an industrial or 'offensive' nature. The resort's popularity gave it grand hotels such as the Scarisbrick and the Prince of Wales, both still standing. Plaques to Sutton can be found at the end of Lord Street, near the junction with Duke Street.

Places of Interest in the Neighbourhood
45. A Wooden Church
47. The Night of the Green Sea
48. Lancashire's Biggest Draught Excluder

47.   The Night of the Green Sea

Position: Lytham St. Annes and Southport
O.S.Map: Landranger, Liverpool, Sheet 108
Map Ref: Various sites - use town centre maps
Access: There are promenade monuments at St. Annes and Southport
and cemetery memorials at Lytham and Southport.

December 9th 1886 is one of the most tragic dates in the history of the
lifeboat movement. The German cargo boat *Mexico* had run aground
off the Lancashire coast in a storm and was fast breaking up when
lifeboats at Southport, St. Annes and Lytham were launched. Spec-
tators' worst fears, raised by lack of the usual light signals from the
lifeboats, were confirmed when the bodies of Southport lifeboatmen
began to be washed up. Morning light revealed the Southport boat *Eliza
Fernley*, keel up, on a sandbank. The implications of the tragedy were
only fully realised when *Laura Janet*, the St. Anne's lifeboat, was also
spotted upturned. The 12 crew of the *Mexico* were finally rescued by the
Lytham boat, but 27 of the 44 lifeboatmen who had set out never
returned, leaving behind 16 widows and 50 orphans.

On the back of a wave of national sympathy a relief fund was set up,
as were several monuments to the disaster. A stone lifeboatman stands
gazing towards the site of the disaster on St. Annes promenade with the
names of the entire crew inscribed beneath him whilst churchyard monuments are found at St. Annes and St. Cuthberts (Lytham) churches. A
communal tomb for six of the Southport crew lies in the Duke Street
Cemetery topped by a broken mast and is complemented by a simpler
obelisk on the promenade which commemorates not only the loss of the
Eliza Fernley but also Southport's new 1888 lifeboat station.

At Marshside Road in Churchtown, Southport, lies the 'Fog Bell',
erected in 1869 to help prevent a repeat of a tragedy when seven local
fishermen out shrimping drowned on the marshes in thick fog. The bell
replaced the foghorn which can now be seen in the Botanic Gardens
Museum in Churchtown.

Places of Interest in the Neighbourhood
45. A Wooden Church
46. The Boulevard where East Meets West
48. Lancashire's Biggest Draught Excluder

*The monument to the lifeboatmen who lost their lives following the
wreck of the* Mexico *in 1886, St Annes promenade.*

48. Lancashire's Biggest Draught Excluder

Position: Rufford village, between Chorley and Southport
O.S.Map: Landranger, Liverpool, Sheet 108
Map Ref: 463 160
Access: Rufford is about 5 kilometres north of Burscough on the A59. Rufford Old Hall is well signposted, next to the main road, just north of the village centre.

Rufford Hall is the beautiful 15th century former home of the Hesketh family, now owned by the National Trust. Although the exterior is of beautifully worked timber and plaster the real curiosity lies within the Great Hall.

The 46 feet long hall was used by the Heskeths for dining and has a magnificent hammerbeam roof. Within it stands an immense draught excluder, once common in such homes, but now the only one of its kind in Lancashire. Carved out of bog oak and seven feet wide and nearly as high, it was used to shield the family from draughts whilst they sat enjoying their food and must have taken several servants to move.

You will also get a chance to visit the collections of arms and armour, tapestry, dolls and the folk museum. Fourteen acres of woodland attached to the house provide ample room for strolling. For the latest opening times and admission prices contact (01704) 821254.

Places of Interest in the Neighbourhood
46. The Boulevard where East Meets West
47. The Night of the Green Sea
49. An Astronomer's Tale

49. An Astronomer's Tale

Position: Bretherton, about 10km west of Leyland on the B5248
O.S.Map: Landranger, Preston and Blackpool, Sheet 102
Map Ref: 463 214
Access: Carr House is just off the A59 - B5248 junction, north-west of Bretherton.

In 1639 curate Jeremiah Horrocks was resident at Carr House and it was here, in the blacked-out room above the front porch, that he made the first ever observation of the transit of Venus in front of the sun. Horrocks was an amateur astronomer who had made painstaking calculations as to the time of the transit. He had rushed home several times from work during that particular day and was finally rewarded during the last few hours of daylight as he observed the planet's shadow on the sinking, burning globe. He died three years later at the age of 23 and his outstanding achievement is recorded on his memorial in Westminster Abbey.

Carr House has other notable features. It is a beautiful example of early 17th century vernacular architecture and the long inscription over the doorway records how the house was built for John Stones by his brothers Thomas and Andrew, a London haberdasher and Amsterdam merchant respectively. The house was almost demolished in 1950 before a Lady Lilford persuaded the Ministry of Works to turn it into the Barry Elder doll museum. The museum collection has since moved on but the house remains in fine condition. It is currently the centre of a business dealing in children's activity toys, and can both be visited by those interested in toys and seen from the road.

Places of Interest in the Neighbourhood
48. Lancashire's Biggest Draught Excluder

50. A Moated Manor House

Position: Goosnargh, north of Preston
O.S.Map: Landranger, Preston and Blackpool, Sheet 102
Map Ref: 556 357
Access: Going east on the B5269, just before entering Goosnargh, a track on the right leads to Chingle Hall. Open to the public.

Chingle Hall is thought to be the oldest domestic brick-built building in the United Kingdom. Even more unusually it is an ancient moated manor house, and was built by the Singleton family in 1260 to a cruciform plan alongside Roman Watling Street.

During the Reformation the Hall's chapel became a site of secret Catholic masses and four priests' hiding holes are still evident. These 'holes in the wall' would have been bricked up with the priest hiding inside. St. John Wall, one of the last priests to be executed because of his religion, was born here in 1620. He was hanged, drawn and quartered at Worcester in 1679 and it is believed his head is hidden somewhere in Chingle Hall.

A number of rooms are still in their original condition. For opening details phone (01772) 861082.

Places of Interest in the Neighbourhood
53. Folklore Farms

51. Bremetennacvm

Position: Ribchester
O.S.Map: Landranger, Blackburn and Burnley, Sheet 103
Map Ref: 650 353
Access: To find the Roman museum go to the southern end of the main
street and turn right. It is near the church.

Although Ribchester is a thriving village it still seems haunted by the
ghost of the Romans. In about AD 79 they established a military
settlement here, Bremetennacvm, which became one of their main
strategic strongholds in the north. It guarded a key river crossing and
the vital Manchester to Carlisle and Ilkley to Kirkham road links.
Many of the auxiliary troops manning the fort were from the Danube
or the Asturias region of Spain and helped found the later civilian
community in the area.

 The only visible reminder of the fort today is a rampart outside the
west gate of the churchyard. Much of the fort was washed away by
a change in the course of the river and the rest is buried under the

The replica of the Roman parade helmet,
the Roman Museum, Ribchester.

church. However, significant parts of the bath houses remain. They are accessed from the southern end of the main street by turning east along the banks of the Ribble. An explanatory board explains the complex system of underground heating. The baths were basically a version of the modern sauna, involving heating and cooling the skin then scraping off the exposed dirt with an instrument known as a stirgil. In the museum a small model reconstructs a cross section of the bath houses. The baths were situated some way away from the main fort so as not to constitute a fire hazard and a timetable existed to segregate female from military and male use.

To the rear of the museum further evidence of Roman settlement is found in the form of granaries. There is also a replica of a spectacular Roman parade helmet uncovered in the river in the late 18th century. Regarded as the best example of a helmet ever found in this country, the original is now in the British Museum.

Places of Interest in the Neighbourhood
52. Elaborate Provision for the Poor
53. Folklore Farms
54. Versailles comes to Lancashire

Stydd Almshouses, Stydd.

52. Elaborate Provision for the Poor

Position: Stydd village, just north of Ribchester
O.S.Map: Landranger, Blackburn and Burnley, Sheet 103
Map Ref: 654 361
Access: Five minutes walk from Ribchester. Head east out of
Ribchester on the B6245 and go left up Stydd Lane.

Stydd almshouses immediately strike you with their surreal architecture and idyllic setting. The main body of the building resembles a
traditional Lancashire house, but the pillared façade is clearly based
on an elaborate Italian design. The loggia (a gallery with sides open to
the air) allows residents to sit out under the arched canopy. The
almshouses have been restored and are still used.

Their modest size reflects the fact they were established by a lesser
member of the local Shireburn aristocracy, John Shireburn. They were
founded under his will in 1726. Although the almshouses in nearby
Hurst Green (map ref: 684 384), also established by the Shireburns, are
grander in scale they lack the remarkable blend of style of their Stydd
counterparts.

The ambience of this quiet little corner is enhanced by the nearby
Church of St. Saviour's, further up the track. It is based on a 12th
century barn church and housed a minor community of the Knights
Templar, rich and powerful religious knights who fought in the
Crusades.

Places of Interest in the Neighbourhood
51. Bremetennacvm
53. Folklore Farms
54. Versailles comes to Lancashire

53. Folklore Farms

Position: East of Longridge.
O.S.Map: Landranger, Blackburn and Burnley, Sheet 103
Map Ref: Written Stone Farm, 626 379
Access: Written Stone Farm is on an unmade track, just north of the B6243, two to three kilometres to the east of Longridge centre. It is marked on the map as a non-Roman antiquity. Cow Rib Farm is between Longridge and Whittingham to the west, approximately a quarter of a mile west-north-west of the Catholic church in Longridge.

Lancashire seems to have more than its fair share of folklore in the form of boggarts (cunning spirits with individual personalities) and witches. Both have left traces of their reputation behind them near Longridge. Standing outside Written Stone Farm look in the high verge by the farm gate to discover an eight feet long piece of gritstone bearing the inscription 'Rafe Radcliffe laid this stone to lye for ever'. This is supposedly the grave of a notorious local boggart who was interred here in 1655. The stone was moved once, but the change seemed to prompt accidents so it was returned to its original resting place. Before his death, the boggart was said to taunt travellers by pinching and punching them.

At Halfpenny Lane, Longridge lies Dun Cow Rib (or Owd Cow Rib) Farmhouse. Look beneath the coat of arms above the doorway to see a large cow rib. According to local tradition this is the rib of an enormous dun cow that appeared during a severe drought. The local people drank a seemingly unstoppable supply of milk from its udders and pronounced on its miraculous appearance and magically endless milk supply. The cow was later found dead, milked dry, allegedly killed by the hands of Mag Shelton, a Fylde witch who had taken to wandering far away from her home town.

Places of Interest in the Neighbourhood
50. A Moated Manor House
51. Bremetennacvm
52. Elaborate Provision for the Poor

54. Versailles comes to Lancashire

Position: Hurst Green village
O.S.Map: Landranger, Blackburn and Burnley, Sheet 103
Map Ref: 690 391
Access: Approached from the village of Hurst Green via a minor road which gives a splendid view of the façade of Stonyhurst College. House and gardens open in July and August.

The local landowners in the Hurst Green area constructed this magnificent house in the late 16th century. The long driveway, which is also a minor road, is surely one of the most impressive approaches to any building in the country. Constructed by the Shireburn family, the most important gentry in the Ribble Valley, it was given to the Society of Jesus, better known as the Jesuits, in 1794. These radicals of the Catholic faith had been expelled from their original home in northern France and moved to Stonyhurst to practise their faith.

The Jesuits were responsible for the addition of the Church of St. Peter, a replica of King's College, Cambridge. The college houses some ancient relics, including a 7th century copy of the Gospel of St. John which St. Cuthbert held in his hands on his deathbed and was originally buried with him in his coffin. Equally priceless is a velvet cape with a Tudor Rose on it, taken to the Field of the Cloth of Gold by Henry VIII. There is also a lot to admire in the grounds; two long

Stonyhurst College, Hurst Green.

pools flank the approach up the main drive and a Roman altar discovered at Ribchester lies in the gardens.

Today it is a Catholic boys' school and guided tours in the summer holidays take in the library, chapel, schoolrooms and historic apartments. Even when closed to the public the network of footpaths surrounding the college are worth exploring, and provide good views of the façade, a domed observatory and the rear of the gardens. Phone (01254) 826345 for more details.

Places of Interest in the Neighbourhood
51. Bremetennacvm
52. Elaborate Provision for the Poor
55. A Viaduct in Praise of a Monastery
56. Immortalised in Alabaster

Whalley viaduct.

55. A Viaduct in Praise of a Monastery

Position: Whalley
O.S.Map: Landranger, Blackburn and Burnley, Sheet 103
Map Ref: 728 364
Access: Head down 'The Sands' off the main road in Whalley. Pass the abbey on the left and go through the gatehouse, to the aqueduct.

The remains of Whalley Abbey dominate the approach to this curiosity but you must pass under the viaduct to see the designer's own tribute to the imposing ruins. The infilled arches flanking the main arch show an impressive gothic design that echoes the dominant architectural style of the medieval abbey, of which little remains. The last abbot, William Paslew, was hanged in 1537 for providing help to participants in the Pilgrimage of Grace, a northern protest against Henry VIII's policies. Much of the abbey was ransacked after the Dissolution of the Monasteries by a local family, the Asshetons, but the grounds provide a lovely setting for wandering by the River Calder.

From the hill known as 'The Nab', to the south of Whalley, on Moor Lane you can see the viaduct's forty eight arches, made of seven million bricks. It was built in 1850 to carry the Blackburn-Clitheroe line sixty five feet above the River Calder. The line is still in use today.

Places of Interest in the Neighbourhood
23. A Rare Relic of Norman Agriculture
24. In Roman Footsteps
25. A Fêted Son
56. Immortalised in Alabaster

56. Immortalised in Alabaster

Position: Great Mitton village, north of Whalley
O.S.Map: Landranger, Blackburn and Burnley, Sheet 103
Map Ref: 715 389
Access: All Hallows Church is just off the B6246, the main road
passing through Great Mitton. Often locked during the week; if so
obtain the key from the verger at the house by the church gate.

The Shireburns were an aristocratic family that liked to do things in
style. They were responsible for the magnificent Stonyhurst College, as
well as Stydd and Hurst Green almshouses (see numbers 52 and 54).
They also left behind the magnificent collection of recumbent effigies in
the family chapel at All Hallows, Great Mitton.

Family shrines are not uncommon but it is unusual to find 6 members of the same family represented together. The collective effect is
remarkable, as several generations of the Shireburns are reunited in
serenity. The most dominant effigies are those of Richard Shireburn
and his wife Maud, who lie romantically side by side, he in full armour
and she in delicate petticoats. Richard had the misfortune to die in the
same year the 13th century chapel was rebuilt in 1544. Beneath them
are carvings of their children and the coats of arms of the families
the Shireburns married into. The saddest monument, against the west
wall, is to a later Richard Shireburn who died in 1702, aged 9, after
eating poisonous berries. He is depicted with a skull and crossbones
and weeping cherubs.

Places of Interest in the Neighbourhood
23. A Rare Relic of Norman Agriculture
24. In Roman Footsteps
54. Versailles Comes to Lancashire
55. A Viaduct in Praise of a Monastery

57. A Small but Serious Castle

Position: Clitheroe
O.S.Map: Landranger, Blackburn and Burnley, Sheet 103
Map Ref: 743 416
Access: The main entrance to the Castle is at the southern end of
Castle Street, two minutes walk from the town centre. Free admission.

Clitheroe Castle's claim to fame is that it has one of the smallest stone
keeps of any castle in the country. It is also one of the last standing
castles in the county to be garrisoned by the Royalists during the Civil
War.

The keep can be seen high on a limestone knoll. Together with the
former Steward's House it forms the only substantial remains of a once
numerous group of buildings. Internally the rooms of the keep would
have measured about twenty feet square, although what now remains

The remains of Clitheroe Castle.

is largely a roofless shell. The Castle's small scale was probably due to several factors. During its construction in the 12th century the Blackburnshire area was relatively poor and resources were scarce. Even more significantly, in the days before gunpowder, a strong strategic position such as Clitheroe Castle's was more important than massive defences.

Built by the Norman De Lacys, the Castle was an impressive regional centre for the Honour of Clitheroe, a territorial unit stretching from Slaidburn to Bury. It contained a gaol, chapel and stables as well as the administrative buildings. The original wall enclosing the bailey (the outer court of the castle) is still evident in places. It was occupied by a Royalist garrison during the Civil War, and though its destruction was ordered by Parliament after the war it is unclear to what extent man, as opposed to the ravages of time, was responsible for its subsequent decay. Although partly repaired in 1848 it never recovered its former glory. It remained the centre of local government until the early 19th century and in 1919 was sold by the then owner, Lord Montague of Beaulieu, to the people of Clitheroe, becoming a memorial for the town's war dead.

Places of Interest in the Neighbourhood
56. Immortalised in Alabaster
58. A Little Piece of Westminster
59. Medieval Rubbish

58. A Little Piece of Westminster

Position: Castle Gardens, near Clitheroe town centre
O.S.Map: Landranger, Blackburn and Burnley, Sheet 103
Map Ref: 742 415
Access: The Castle Gardens and Turret Monument are ten minutes walk from the main street. Admission free.

At first sight the stone turret in the rose garden beneath the Steward's House appears to be little more than decorative. Closer inspection of one of its two plaques reveals that it was once part of the parapet of the Houses of Parliament. It was presented to the Borough of Clitheroe by Captain Sir William Brass, the town's MP from 1922 until his death in 1945, who also paid for the surrounding garden to celebrate the Coronation of George VI in 1937.

Places of Interest in the Neighbourhood
56. Immortalised in Alabaster
57. A Small but Serious Castle
59. Medieval Rubbish

The stone turret from the Houses of Parliament, Clitheroe Castle.

59. Medieval Rubbish

Position: Sawley village, north east of Clitheroe
O.S.Map: Landranger, Blackburn and Burnley, Sheet 103
Map Ref: 776 465
Access: The Abbey lies at the centre of Sawley village, next to the main street. It is in the care of English Heritage and is open; Good Friday to September 30th daily, 10 a.m. till 1 p.m. and 2 p.m. till 6 p.m. 1st October to Maundy Thursday daily, 10 a.m. till 1 p.m. and 2 p.m. till 4 p.m. Closed Mondays and public holidays at Christmas and New Year.

Whilst several crumbling stone walls of this Cistercian abbey remain, the most eye-catching feature is the small series of arches set over what appears to be a sunken pavement on the far side of the grounds. This was the main drain for the Abbey, down which the river was diverted to carry away refuse. The church and the dormitory's substantial remains are grouped around the original staircase.

   In historical terms Sawley was neither rich or large. After its foundation in 1148 it suffered from competition at the hands of nearby Whalley Abbey (see entry 55). After the Dissolution the monks were reinstated in the Abbey, but its last abbot was executed in the wake of the Pilgrimage of Grace and the buildings fell into decline.

Places of Interest in the Neighbourhood
57. A Small but Serious Castle
58. A Little Piece of Westminster

A view of the main drain at Sawley Abbey.

60. The Windmill by the Sea

Position: Lytham St. Annes and Thornton
O.S.Map: Landranger, Preston and Blackpool, Sheet 102
Map Ref: 371 271 and 335 426
Access: Lytham windmill is on the seafront in front of the A584.
Marsh Mill windmill is near the B5268 to the east of Thornton. Both
are marked with windmill symbols on the Landranger map.

Windmills were once common on the flat plain of the Fylde, but only
two have substantially survived the ravages of time. The windmill at
Lytham stands on Lytham Green, well-placed to catch the prevailing
winds and next to the old lifeboat house. Richard Cookson leased the

Lytham windmill.

land to build this particular mill in 1805. In 1909 a Manchester school-boy on an outing grabbed hold of one of the sails whilst they were in use and plunged to his death after failing to maintain his hold. In 1918 a fire damaged the mill beyond repair and in 1921 a freak gust of wind reversed the sails and wrecked the internal machinery. The local heritage society hold various exhibitions in the windmill although the sails and internal machinery are no longer functional: for details phone Lytham Tourist Office on (01253) 725610.

Marsh Mill windmill appears an even more incongruous addition to the skyline, surrounded as it is by suburban housing. It was built in 1794 by Ralph Slater, a Fylde millwright, and is still in working order. The ground floor houses the Clog Museum, and there is a small charge for a guided tour.

Places of Interest in the Neighbourhood
61. A Saint's Last Resting Place

St Cuthbert's Cross, Lytham St. Annes.

61. A Saint's Last Resting Place

Position: Lytham St. Annes
O.S.Map: Landranger, Preston and Blackpool, Sheet 102
Map Ref: 369 272
Access: St. Cuthbert's Cross is set back in a hedgerow behind Lowther
Gardens, to the east of St. Cuthbert's Church. Within walking distance
of town centre.

The cross of Saint Cuthbert that lies here was originally medieval,
but its more modern replacement was placed in the original ancient
socket in the early 20th century by a local canon in gratitude for his
recovery from illness. It was, however, intended to be a re-creation of
the original and serves as an interesting reminder of one of England's
most venerated saints.

Cuthbert was a childhood visionary who became a legend in his own
lifetime. Soon after his death in 686, on the remote island of Lindisfarne off the Northumbrian coast, pilgrims soon began visiting his
shrine. When Danish invaders later took Lindisfarne by storm the
monks fled, taking St. Cuthbert's remains with them. They kept on the
move for seven years, carrying the saint's remains and erecting crosses
where St. Cuthbert had lain for the night. Eventually they settled
at Chester-le-Street where a great cathedral was built in Cuthbert's
honour.

Places of Interest in the Neighbourhood
60. The Windmill by the Sea

62. A One Horse Town

Position: Singleton village, east of Blackpool
O.S.Map: Landranger, Preston and Blackpool, Sheet 102
Map Ref: 383 382
Access: At the junction of Church Lane and the B5260 in Singleton.

This impressive brick, timber and stucco building was built sometime towards the end of the last century to serve as Singleton's fire station, although it looks too small to be suitable. The first fire brigade in the village was established in 1882, its captain summoning his fourteen men to the station, possibly by ringing a bell in the small tower. The manual fire engine was pulled by a single horse which was kept in a nearby field, leading local wags to joke that by the time the horse had been caught the fire would have gone out or the building been destroyed. It is now one of the country's most unusual electricity sub-stations!

Places of Interest in the Neighbourhood
63. The North's Greatest Landmark
64. Market Square Relics

Singleton fire station.

63. The North's Greatest Landmark

Position: Blackpool
O.S.Map: Landranger, Preston and Blackpool, Sheet 102
Map Ref: 305 360
Access: Head for the seafront in Blackpool and you can't miss the tower! Entrance ticket required to go to the top.

Although it remains one of the country's most famous buildings Blackpool Tower caused a real sensation when it opened in 1894. Of the 70,000 who turned up for the official opening only a few thousand managed to make it to one of the viewing platforms or to the circus and ballroom located between its four huge feet. The ballroom itself is a piece of elaborate rococo architecture, complete with luxuriously decorated domes and gilded plasterwork. A giant wheel was opened alongside two years later but was dismantled in 1928.

An unashamed copy of the 1889 Eiffel Tower, Blackpool Tower boasts some awesome statistics. In its original form the 518 feet high

Blackpool Tower.

tower incorporated 2,493 tons of steel, and in a 70 mph wind the top has a one inch sway. 1900 saw the opening of the Tower Ballroom, still synonymous with the song 'I Do Like to be Beside the Seaside', played on the organ by Reginald Dixon. A 1901 guide lists an aquarium, menagerie, monkey house, aviary, bear pits, roof gardens and an old English village. The principal attractions were changed regularly and included the Midget Town, inhabited by human midgets, and exhibitions of flying, during which early biplanes circled the tower.

The tower survived a fire in the ballroom in 1956 which threatened to melt the iron legs, and in 1961 it was given a new front as part of a scheme to modernize the promenade. During the First World War it was temporarily used for assembling silk parachutes, whilst during the Second World War a Fleetwood councillor suggested pulling it down on the grounds that it was too obvious a target for the enemy. Today it is owned by the First Leisure Corporation, a single ticket giving entry to all the traditional features, including a ride up in the lift to the viewing platform, which in turn provides spectacular views of the Welsh mountains, Cumbrian hills, the Pennines, the gas rigs in the Irish Sea, and occasionally the Isle of Man.

Places of Interest in the Neighbourhood
62. A One Horse Town
64. Market Square Relics

64. Market Square Relics

Position: Poulton-le-Fylde
O.S.Map: Landranger, Preston and Blackpool, Sheet 102.
Map Ref: 347 395
Access: The relics are near St. Chad's Church, five minutes from the station.

Although market place relics are not uncommon it is quite unusual to find such a varied collection in one spot. The market place at Poulton-le-Fylde, the hub of the village in medieval times, houses a fine collection.

Surrounding a well-preserved market cross are stocks, a whipping post, and a fish-stone - where fishmongers from Blackpool once sold

The Market Place at Poulton-le-Fylde, showing the fish-stone and whipping post.

their wares. Although the whipping post is now without its manacles, records show that neither it nor the stocks were placed here as an idle threat. In 1629 Elizabeth Johnson and Jane Clark were placed in the stocks, being described as 'wandering persons' and accused of stealing clothes. In 1648 Jonathan Bell and John Swift were publicly whipped for 'divers, notorious misdemeanors'.

Places of Interest in the Neighbourhood
62. A One Horse Town
63. The North's Greatest Landmark

An 18th century milestone near Garstang.

65. When is a Mile not a Mile?

Position: The turnpike milestones at Garstang are found on the A6, to the south and north of the town
O.S.Map: Landranger, Preston and Blackpool, Sheet 102
Map Ref: The best examples are north of Barton (514 384 approximately)
Access: Right next to the A6 at numerous places.

At the side of the A6 near Garstang stand turnpike milestones marking the course of the old turnpike road that ran north from Preston. A mile walked on the turnpike would have taken longer in the 18th century than it does today, as the miles measured by the markers are significantly longer than the modern mile. In the days of the turnpikes the length of a mile was established by tradition and a standard mile was not defined until Victorian times. South of Garstang the mileposts are circular with their destinations inscribed in elegant 'handwritten' lettering, whilst to the north they are triangular with Roman style inscriptions.

A junction marker at Dunsop Bridge (map ref: 657 501), made of stone and dated 1739, has been used as the base for a late 19th century fingerpost. Notice how the lower figures are longer for equivalent distances, indicating the use of the traditionally longer mile. Such stones, showing distances to the nearest market town had to be erected after an Act of Parliament of 1738.

66. The Lighthouse of the Pharos

Position: Fleetwood
O.S.Map: Landranger, Preston and Blackpool, Sheet 102
Map Ref: 339 484 and 338 486
Access: The Pharos Lighthouse is set just back from the front whilst the octagonal lighthouse is within walking distance on the north-west corner of the Fleetwood peninsula (both marked by appropriate Landranger symbols).

The architect Decimus Burton, designer of Fleetwood, clearly had an interest in exotic constructions; although the Chinese pavilion he built has long since disappeared the Pharos lighthouse, based on the ancient Egyptian lighthouse at Alexandria, remains in all its glory. Its tall sandstone column is in complete contrast to the smaller neighbouring lighthouse he also designed, and whose octagonal tower and colonnaded base are altogether more flamboyant. Their lights, when viewed from the sea, are set at different heights, allowing ships to use the offset alignment of the two to navigate the Wyre channel.

Despite their striking architecture the lighthouses were essentially practical constructions. Their gas lights were first lit in 1840, shortly after Fleetwood's foundation in the 1830's. Their design reflects Burton's innovative influence (he also designed the Wellington Arch at Hyde Park Corner), combined with the ambition of the man who conceived and financed Fleetwood's birth, Sir Peter Hesketh-Fleetwood. It was Burton who laid out Fleetwood's wide streets, radiating outwards from Tup Hill, and was responsible for the grand Euston Hotel, near the lower lighthouse. Its name consciously mirrored that of the London station as Fleetwood was then on the rail and sea routes from London to Glasgow. Hesketh-Fleetwood's new town, planned as both resort and commercial port, originally boomed, but his grand ambitions and the immense capital required finally forced him to sell off his estates to pay his creditors, and in due course Fleetwood's fortunes became eclipsed by those of Blackpool.

Decimus Burton's Lower Lighthouse, Fleetwood.

67. The Maritime Monks

Position: About 10 miles south of Lancaster
O.S.Map: Landranger, Preston and Blackpool, Sheet 102
Map Ref: 428 537
Access: On minor roads from the A588. Final approach on foot.
Parking difficult in the immediate area so it is best to park in the village
of Glasson and follow the Lancashire Coastal Way on foot for 4
kilometres or so.

A bleak and forbidding spot on the Lancastrian coast marks where a
12th century hermit founded a leper hospital. Originally the building
stood on an island, surrounded by treacherous salt marshes. In 1190
Cockersand Abbey was founded on the same spot, its monks battling
with high tides which washed away much of their work. By the 15th
century it was one of the three richest abbeys in Lancashire. The surrounding marshland had been drained, a quay built, and the first lighthouse on this part of the coast may well have been in operation.

Today the only part remaining virtually intact is the Chapter House,
where the monks once gathered daily to discuss a chapter from 'The
Rule', the strict code which governed their lives. After the Reformation a
local aristocratic family, the Daltons, destroyed most of the Abbey but
turned the Chapter House into a family mausoleum. If the door is open
you may enter to discover a beautiful octagonal room with intricate
carving. It is thought the carved Renaissance chest and 14th century
choir stalls in Lancaster Priory may have come from the Abbey.

Places of Interest in the Neighbourhood
68. Stately Resting Places

The remains of Cockersand Abbey.

68. Stately Resting Places

Position: Churchyards at Thurnham and Halton
O.S.Map: Landranger, Preston and Blackpool, Sheet 102 and
Landranger, Kendal to Morecambe, Sheet 97
Map Ref: 465 543 and 498 647
Access: Thurnham churchyard is 15 minutes walk from the village of
Upper Thurnham. Halton church is next to the main road in the village.

Two grand but very different family mausoleums are found in north-
west Lancashire. The mausoleum at the Church of St. Thomas and St.
Elizabeth in Upper Thurnham was built for the staunchly Catholic
Gillow family and is distinctly Egyptian, most noticeably on the four
columns of the southern side with their papyrus decoration. It was
built in about 1830 and is the final resting place of five members of
the family. They are best known for their association with furniture

Bradshaw Mausoleum, Halton.

making and fine examples of their craft can be seen at their home, Leighton Hall (map ref: 494 744).

The Bradshaw family mausoleum built into the wall behind Halton church is a much grander, though more dilapidated affair. It seems consciously modelled on a house façade, although the central doorway has been blocked up and urns decorate the openings at either side. The slate roof has collapsed onto the stone barrel vault below. The Bradshaws were the lords of the manor from 1743.

Places of Interest in the Neighbourhood
67. The Maritime Monks
70. A Grand Engineering Feat
71. The Taj Mahal of the North
72. The Garden House in a Town Centre
73. Monument to an Age

Claughton Hall, near Claughton.

69. Moving House

Position: The edge of Claughton Moor, south-east of Claughton
village
O.S.Map: Landranger, Kendal to Morecambe, Sheet 97
Map Ref: 572 661
Access: Take the minor road opposite the Fenwick Arms in Claughton
and keep to the right to go through a gate onto a track. Climb the
track for less than a kilometre for a view of Claughton Hall.

To Edmund Morse, moving house clearly meant something quite different than to the rest of us. He employed a local architect to dismantle
Claughton Hall and move it 300 feet up the hillside from its original
site in the bottom of the Lune valley. The whole task took from 1932 to
1935. Morse actually left behind one wing of the house, which still
stands alone by the old church.

Nowadays most people pass Claughton Hall for the fine views of the
Lune valley and the Lakeland fells. Few realise the imposing twin-
towered hall is the former 17th century residence of the Croft family,
moved up here brick by brick on an industrialist's whim. Morse's
reasons for doing so remain unclear; he may have wanted to reflect
what he felt was his own prestige (he was managing director of
Williamsons, the late Lord Ashton's company (see 71)), or he may just
have wanted to give the house a view!

Places of Interest in the Neighbourhood
74. Enigmatic Crosses
78. A Gamekeeper's Retreat

The Lune aqueduct, Lancaster.

70. A Grand Engineering Feat

Position: Across the Lune, on the north-eastern edge of Lancaster
O.S.Map: Landranger, Kendal to Morecambe, Sheet 97
Map Ref: 483 638
Access: Via the Lune walk/cycle way from the southern side, or the minor road on the north side. You can walk across the Lune aqueduct on the towpath from either side.

Greeted as an extraordinary engineering achievement on its opening in 1797, the Lune aqueduct is still impressive. Its five massively solid arches stretch some 600 feet across the river, and its stone piers are supported by 20 feet long wooden piles sunk into the river bed. Doric columns break up the sturdy lines of the cornice that crowns the arches. On the Lancaster side of the aqueduct two lines of Latin attest to the fact the canal it carries linked two once-remote places, Preston and Kendal, creating new sources of wealth. An English inscription on the other side simply states 'To Public Prosperity'.

The aqueduct's engineer was John Rennie (1761-1821), a millwright without any formal qualifications who went on to become one of the pioneers of the canal age and was also the driving force behind many of London's bridges, as well as the East India Docks and Bell Rock Lighthouse.

Places of Interest in the Neighbourhood
71. The Taj Mahal of the North
72. The Garden House in a Town Centre
73. Monument to an Age

71. The Taj Mahal of the North

Position: Lancaster
O.S.Map: Landranger, Kendal to Morecambe, Sheet 97
Map Ref: 493 614
Access: The memorial is in the east of Lancaster, between the town centre and the M6. It is well signposted from M6 junctions 33 or 34 and from the centre. Open all year round. A charge is made to the viewing gallery.

What is arguably England's grandest folly is also one of its most visible. The Ashton Memorial stands 120 feet high and has an elaborate 50 feet staircase leading to its main entrance. With its imposing central dome and beautiful, white Portland stone masonry it is not difficult to see why it has been nicknamed the Taj Mahal of the North. Opened in 1909, it was the brainchild of local entrepreneur Lord Ashton and was constructed as a tribute to his family. There are wonderful views from the viewing platform, and the surrounding attractions include a butterfly garden and a display about the family.

Initially a patron of many local charities, Lord Ashton spent more than half a million pounds on good works. He was known as the 'lino king' and was Lancaster's greatest benefactor, but towards the end of his life he became increasingly bitter. Politically a Liberal, he could not reconcile himself to the demands of his workforce for better pay and conditions. His donations to good causes stopped, and he died in 1930 a virtual recluse.

Places of Interest in the Neighbourhood
70. A Grand Engineering Feat
72. The Garden House in a Town Centre
73. Monument to an Age
74. Enigmatic Crosses
76. A Grave Concern
77. An Epic Hotel

The Ashton Memorial, Lancaster.

The Music Room, Lancaster.

72. The Garden House in a Town Centre

Position: Lancaster town centre
O.S.Map: Landranger, Kendal to Morecambe, Sheet 97. Lancaster town centre map available from the tourist information office
Map Ref: 476 618
Access: Sun Street. For a viewing appointment contact the administrator of the Landmark Trust on (01524) 60658.

Looking at the façade of the Music Room you would not immediately realise this was once a summer house used for recitals at the end of a garden. Sun Street has encroached and surrounded this elaborate building with more mundane architecture. Its style is an example of the baroque architecture popular in the 18th century, and the house was built in 1730. The façade has a beautiful entry arch but the plaster-work of the interior is the real glory. The Greek theme of the exterior is continued as the Muses of Astronomy, Amorous Poetry, Comedy, Dancing, Eloquence, History, Music, Rhetoric and Tragedy are all depicted. These nine muses were sister goddesses, the offspring of Zeus and Mnemosyne (Memory), considered the inspirers of learning and the arts. Also look out for Apollo, the sun god and Ceres, the goddess of agriculture.

Places of Interest in the Neighbourhood
70. A Grand Engineering Feat
71. The Taj Mahal of the North
73. Monument to an Age
74. Enigmatic Crosses
76. A Grave Concern
77. An Epic Hotel

73. Monument to an Age

Position: Dalton Square, Lancaster
O.S.Map: Landranger, Kendal to Morecambe, Sheet 97. Town centre map useful
Map Ref: 479 615
Access: Train access to town centre as well as central parking.

The statue of Queen Victoria in Dalton Square, Lancaster, is a monument to an era. Victoria's lofty presence is flanked by four lions, whilst the four sides of the weighty plinth carry carvings of an array of eminent Victorians. Freedom, justice, wisdom and truth are found on the plinth corners in the form of seated women surrounded by angels and putti. The monument was given to the town of Lancaster by Lord Ashton in 1906 (see 71).

As well as household names such as Dickens, Florence Nightingale and Gladstone, numerous scientists, artists and politicians are represented - including Benjamin Franklin, Isaac Pitman, General Gordon, Rowland Hill and Lord Macaulay. There is also a family connection in two of the figures; James Williamson was Lord Ashton's father and Viscount Peel was his son-in-law. The nearby Town Hall, together with the statue, cost Lord Ashton over £155,000.

Places of Interest in the Neighbourhood
70. A Grand Engineering Feat
71. The Taj Mahal of the North
72. The Garden House in a Town Centre
74. Enigmatic Crosses
76. A Grave Concern
77. An Epic Hotel

The statue of Queen Victoria, Lancaster.

One of the ancient crosses in Whalley churchyard.

74. Enigmatic Crosses

Position: Halton village
O.S.Map: Landranger, Kendal to Morecambe, Sheet 97
Map Ref: 498 647
Access: Halton church is next to the main road through the village.

One of the most curious of Lancashire's ancient crosses lies in Halton churchyard. Dating from the 11th century, it mixes both Christian and Norse 'pagan' motifs. On one side of the lower part the Cross and the Risen Christ are clearly carved whilst two other sides show a horse and an intricate Scandinavian pattern. Most fascinating is the remaining side, which depicts scenes from the Norse saga of Sigurd, a tale of good over evil, somewhat anglicised and Christianised here. The cross is also a fascinating testimony to the state of the church in this area before the arrival of the Normans, to whom such co-existence of beliefs would have been less acceptable. Such crosses were relatively common in Anglo Saxon England and served a variety of purposes, from boundary markers to meeting places and centres for worship.

Even more mysterious crosses are to be found in Whalley churchyard (map ref: 733 362). The two best preserved stand on the southern side of Whalley church and probably date from the 9th to the 11th centuries. They show strong elements of Celtic design, and may be associated with Saints Augustus and Paulinus. Prior to 1066 Whalley had been the centre of a vast parish, stretching thirty miles from the Bowland plateau to the Cliviger watershed in the South Pennines, with locals gathering at wayside preaching crosses to worship. However, the Norman invaders carved out new parishes at Blackburn, Mitton and Slaidburn and used their wealth to found several churches, making many such crosses obsolete.

Places of Interest in the Neighbourhood
69. Moving House
70. A Grand Engineering Feat
71. The Taj Mahal of the North
72. The Garden House in a Town Centre
73. Monument to an Age

75. A Politically Incorrect Epitaph

Position: Sunderland Point
O.S.Map: Landranger, Preston and Blackpool, Sheet 102
Map Ref: 425 561
Access: Sunderland is reached by a road running across salt marshes from Overton. In Sunderland go down The Lane to the west shore and turn left to reach Sambo's Grave. The road is often submerged at high tide, so any visit should be timed accordingly.

Sunderland is a ghost port which declined in the late 18th century as its rival ports on the other side of the Lune, Lancaster and Glasson, grew. It was largely the brainchild of Robert Lawson, a Lancaster merchant, who wanted to exploit the growing trade with the West Indies and who was one of the first importers of cotton. The port area has remained virtually fossilised since its decline and all that remains today are a few houses, Lawson's quay and a single Georgian gatepier.

The most touching reminder of the West Indian trade is the grave of a black man, 'Poor Sambo', which is still well-tended and strewn with flowers. It seems Sambo was a slave who accompanied his master from the West Indies and died in Sunderland. Being a pagan, he was denied a burial in consecrated ground and ended up in the rabbit warren behind the inn. It was only later, in the 18th century, that a retired schoolmaster discovered the story of the slave and made a memorial collection. He also wrote an elegy to 'Poor Sambo' and was responsible for the poetic epitaph you see on his grave. Whilst 'Sambo' is widely regarded as a derogatory term today, it was clearly used sympathetically in this case.

Places of Interest in the Neighbourhood
76. A Grave Concern
77. An Epic Hotel

76. A Grave Concern

Position: Heysham, west of Lancaster
O.S.Map: Landranger, Kendal to Morecambe, Sheet 97
Map Ref: 411 617
Access: The ancient rock-hewn graves lie next to Saint Patrick's
Chapel in Heysham, on the cliff edge. For other locations see below.

Near the ruins of Saint Patrick's Chapel at Heysham lie the remains
of some unusual rock-hewn Saxon graves on an impressive cliff-top
site. Although the graves have been uncovered it is not known who
they were for, although they are associated with the nearby 9th century chapel. Note the chiselled hole above where the head would have
lain, presumably to take a cross. Legend has it that Saint Patrick was
responsible for the building of the chapel after being shipwrecked here.
It was made of limestone blocks fused together by molten shells. The
cliff-top site also boasts fantastic views across the water to Furness
and the Lakeland Fells. Inside the adjacent Saint Peter's Church is a

The Saxon graves near the ruins of St. Patrick's Chapel, Heysham.

beautifully decorated Viking 10th century 'hogback' tombstone, showing men and animals in a scene from a Norse saga.

Near the east gate of St. James' Church at Haslingden is a gravestone (map ref: 785 236) paying poetic tribute to Christopher Duckworth, who spent many of his 56 years tending his master's packhorses. William Walker's grave at St. Andrew's Parish Church in Leyland has probably the oldest gravestone in the county. Dated 1588, it takes the form of a stone slab on a low stone base and bears a primitively incised figure of a man.

Churchyards are also popular places for monuments recording the death of those who are buried elsewhere. One of the most poignant is that to the Stott Milne family at St. Bartholomew's in Whitworth (see 1), whose six children all died in infancy, at ages ranging from seven weeks and fifteen months. Two contrasting monuments can be found at St. James' Church in Accrington, one to the famous 'Accrington Pals' (see 8) and the other to the local Peel family, who produced the 19th century prime minister.

Places of Interest in the Neighbourhood
71. The Taj Mahal of the North
72. The Garden House in a Town Centre
73. Monument to an Age
77. An Epic Hotel

77. An Epic Hotel

Position: Morecambe, opposite the railway station, on the front
O.S.Map: Landranger, Kendal to Morecambe, Sheet 97
Map Ref: 427 641
Access: Have a drink at the Midland Hotel then see the sculptures.

The curving white façade of the Midland Hotel is instantly recognisable as dating from this century (1933). For the hotel's really striking features, three unusual carvings by the well-known sculptor Eric Gill, you must go inside. All have a suitably maritime flavour. The bas-relief on the ceiling of the staircase tower depicts the sea god Triton and mermaids. In the Eric Gill suite there is a large carved map of Morecambe Bay along with a more recent depiction of a scene from Homer's Odyssey, showing the Greek hero Odysseus being welcomed by Princess Nausicaa.

The building itself was constructed by the London, Midland and Scottish Railway and reflects the growth of the resort after the First World War, despite a serious economic depression in the 1920s. For example, 1933 also saw the opening of the ornamental gardens and the spur promenade around the hotel, whilst the harbour bandstand and band area were opened in 1934.

Places of Interest in the Neighbourhood
71. The Taj Mahal of the North
72. The Garden House in a Town Centre
73. Monument to an Age
76. A Grave Concern

78. A Gamekeeper's Retreat

Position: Near the small village of Capernwray, north-east of
Carnforth.
O.S.Map: Landranger, Kendal to Morecambe, Sheet 97
Map Ref: 542 714
Access: Just east of Capernwray a little used footpath (muddy in
winter) leads near Hobson's Caravan Park and to the Gamekeeper's
Tower. Tower and footpath are marked on the Landranger Map.

This eerie gothic tower stands on a natural vantage point looking out
over the surrounding countryside. It was built by the owner of nearby
Capernwray Hall as a lookout tower for his gamekeeper.
   Today it lies semi-ruined, despite being a listed building. Capernwray
Hall was built by the Marton family in the 1830s, but death duties
forced its sale in 1946 and it is now a Christian Conference centre.

Places of Interest in the Neighbourhood
69. Moving House
79. A Defence against the Scots

The Gamekeeper's Tower, Capernwray.

79. A Defence against the Scots

Position: Between Arnside and Silverdale
O.S.Map: Landranger, Kendal to Morecambe, Sheet 97
Map Ref: 458 768
Access: Arnside Tower is visible from the minor road between
Silverdale and Arnside passing to the south-east of Arnside Knott.

This romantically sited ruin is in fact an ancient pele tower, constructed in 1340 with the intention of defending the area against much
feared Scottish raids and incursions by sea pirates. Such raids were
then common in the wake of Robert the Bruce's crushing victory over
Edward II at Bannockburn. Although restored after a fire in 1602, a
storm in 1884 felled one corner and it has since deteriorated to its
current crumbling state.

Pele towers were designed to be residences in times of peace with the
ability to be transformed into mini-fortresses should the Scots mount
a raid. The ground floor, containing store rooms and dairy, was
bypassed by stairs to the first floor. The thick defensive wall had
latrines and huge fireplaces built into it. In medieval times a wooden
stockade would have surrounded the tower to provide extra defences
and house livestock.

Places of Interest in the Neighbourhood
78. A Gamekeeper's Retreat

Arnside Tower.

80. The Forest Courts

Position: Slaidburn village in the Forest of Bowland
O.S.Map: Landranger, Blackburn and Burnley, Sheet 103
Map Ref: 713 525
Access: Upstairs at the Hark to Bounty Inn. Viewing by request at the bar.

Wandering round Slaidburn today it is hard to imagine that this sleepy village was the administrative centre for the whole of the Forest of Bowland. The best reminder of the village's past lies upstairs at the Hark to Bounty Inn where the original panelled courtroom, complete with its dock and witness box, can still be found.

In Norman times Slaidburn was a village in the Lord's Demesne (part of the Honour of Clitheroe), meaning it was held directly by the main lord in the area and was thus of considerable importance. The Forest of Bowland was originally a hunting forest used only by nobility and royalty, and the deer were protected by Forest Law. By the time the court moved to its present site in the 16th century much of the original forest had been given over to cattle, although the court continued in use until as late as 1913.

Places of Interest in the Neighbourhood
57. A Small but Serious Castle
58. A Little Piece of Westminster
59. Medieval Rubbish

Index

The Curiosities of England

The following titles in the series have already been published and can be ordered at all bookshops, or in case of difficulties direct from the publishers.